Pretty
Good
Catholic

Pretty Good Catholic

How to find, date, and marry someone who shares your faith

RACHEL HOOVER CANTO

VIANNEY VOCATIONS

Vianney Vocations, Tallahassee, Florida
© Rachel Hoover Canto
All rights reserved. Published 2024
Printed in the United States of America

ISBN: 979-8-9873125-7-5
LCCN: 2024930805

Cover design by Sam Alzheimer

To my parents, for giving me life
and teaching me that marriage lasts until death.

And to Enrique,
mi prometido. Usque ad mortem.

Contents

Introduction

Something is wrong with Catholic dating culture. If you picked up this book, you're probably experiencing it yourself: you ache to be married, but it seems like there just aren't enough good Catholics out there to marry.

My female friends say that all the men they meet are either religious and chaste, or interesting and attractive, but not both. They find an appealing Hinge profile that says "Catholic," but learn on the first date that he hasn't been to Mass in years. Meanwhile, the men at their parishes every Sunday seem awkward and unwilling to pursue them. One woman who responded to an anonymous survey listed these unattractive qualities in the men around her: "having no friends, not being passionate about anything that isn't directly related to Catholicism, and being socially awkward." She's far from alone.

But men say nearly the same thing: that it's hard to find a woman who's serious about her faith *and* fun to be around. A man answered the same survey saying, "I find a lot of women don't know how to have fun because almost everything is a sin. And that's depressing." Another shared on Reddit that he was ready to "give up on trying to find a woman"—at age twenty-four.

These anecdotes are backed up by marriage statistics. The number of Catholic weddings per year plummeted 77% from 1970 to 2021, according to the Center for Applied Research in the Apostolate—a sharper decline than that of priestly ordinations. Does this decline indicate simply that people are becoming secularized—marrying outside the Church, or cohabiting instead of marrying—or something more: a problem with how practicing Catholics date and look for spouses?

A few years ago, observing this decline and feeling frustration with my own prolonged singleness, I began to try to answer this question. I surveyed roughly 300 self-identified practicing Catholics ages 18-39, asking (for those who were single) why they weren't married, or (for those who were married) what had prevented them from marrying sooner. The top reason given was simply, "I haven't found the right person."

But if thousands of Catholics of both sexes are saying they can't find good spouses, why aren't they finding each other? If you're on a college campus with a vibrant Newman center, or in a city with social opportunities for Catholic young adults, it should be easy to meet someone in person, right?

And if you're in a place with a lower population of Catholics, the explosion of dating apps and websites, including several that are specifically for Catholics, should, in theory, make it easier than ever to meet a good Catholic spouse. Just create your profile, add a few filters to make sure you're paired with people who would be a good fit, and wait for the matches to roll in.

Of course, if you've done anything to find a date, online or offline, you're already laughing (or crying). It's not quite that easy. I could probably make a bingo card of common obstacles we Catholics face, even when we do everything possible to meet the right people. It's harder than it sounds to meet them, and when you do, it's hard to get from meeting to a date. And when you do get to a date, it's *very* hard to get all the way through a relationship to the altar.

As I've gone through nearly a decade of dating myself and talked to many others who are on the same journey while researching this book, I've discovered that there's no one reason why so many Catholics are struggling to find spouses today. Instead, there are countless reasons, all layered one on top of the other.

First, we struggle to understand and send the subtle cues that used to make up the language of appropriate flirtation, which prevents relationships from starting in the first place. One sociable, pretty, and talented woman told me, "You meet a Catholic guy at a party and you're having a great conversation for half an hour . . . and then his girlfriend walks up." Another woman at a Young Catholic Professionals (YCP) conference told me she and her friends meet nice guys all the time, but they just keep chatting at events and never ask them out. More than once, I myself have encountered men who acted friendly and a little flirtatious, but never took even one step to pursue me, though I tried to make it clear I was open to it. (Of course, when I was younger, I thought the ladylike way to behave if I liked a guy was to completely ignore him. Naturally, this didn't get me very far.)

Meanwhile, the men I talked to are baffled from the opposite angle. "How do you tell if a girl's interested?" one male friend asked me in frustration. "Because they act the same either way: smiling and moving their hair . . . I can't tell what they're signaling." Another young man I interviewed for an OSV News article shared, "Sometimes girls drop hints or act interested but guys completely have no idea about this, because they're overthinking: 'Is she dropping a hint or just being friendly?'"

If you're a woman reading this, you might object that the best way to find out is to ask. But countless men, including my interviewee, have told me that they really need to have at least *some* encouragement before asking out a woman. The stakes feel high if they ask someone out and get rejected. Not only is there the normal gut-punch to a man's pride and confidence, he now has to fear asking out any of the woman's friends, because they probably know that she said no to him already.

The Catholic community tends to be tight-knit in a lot of places in the US, whether on college campuses, in small towns, or in cities where the young adults are well connected with each other. So men take a long time to gather information before they ask out the woman who seems most promising. By that point, the woman has started to wonder what's taking him so long and perhaps feels less interested; she wants a man who pursues her with confidence and makes his intentions clear. So the vicious cycle continues.

If two Catholics manage to get into a dating relationship, they run into other problems. There's the constant question, "How far is too far?" when it comes to physical affection. Hopefully, you're dating someone who believes in saving sex for marriage, but there still can be a lot of debate about what other types of touch are okay at what stage of a relationship. One acquaintance of mine used to complain that Catholic guys over-discerned everything, praying for months before even holding a girl's hand. Turning to the Internet for expert advice on the subject doesn't help much, because the experts disagree. Some advocate for zero physical affection for most of the relationship, saying that it creates either a temptation or an undue attachment. On the other hand, some people see nothing wrong with kissing on a first date; after all, kissing isn't sex, and the Church doesn't say it's forbidden. This makes every date a bit of an ordeal: will you have a whole conversation about your physical boundaries right away? That's a lot to talk about with someone you barely know, and yet dodging an unexpected kiss could be even more awkward.

Speaking of discernment, sudden bouts of vocational discernment can derail relationships that appear to be headed for marriage. I met a woman who had been on the receiving end of no fewer than *four* breakups because the men in question decided to discern the priesthood after all. I know plenty of other women (including myself) who have experienced this at least once. These breakups can be particularly hard. A college professor of mine used to say, "You never get over a guy you lose to the seminary." It's an exaggeration, but not completely inaccurate. If you want a holy spouse who does God's will, it's hard to stop feeling affection for someone who is so committed to God's will, even if God's will is apparently leading him or her away from you. And then, if God is really leading him away, why is God hurting *you* so much?

Sometimes, this type of breakup—"It's not you; it's God!"—leads to your own discernment journey. Or a lengthy "season of singleness" sparks self-doubt and questions from well-meaning outsiders. I'll never forget the time a kind older man at church asked me if I would consider becoming a religious sister because, "when a pretty girl like you reaches your age and still isn't married, maybe it's a sign." (I believe I was twenty-four at the time. In his defense, that used to be above the average age for marriage not long ago, though now the average is closer to thirty.) At another point, I had declined to date a man from my parish, and our priest asked me if I had considered the consecrated life. Thinking maybe it was a sign, I went on a discernment journey and dating fast that lasted nearly a year, only to end up deciding on marriage after all, a year older and perhaps a little more desperate.

Then, there are questions like, "How long should we date before getting engaged?" and "How do I know he/she's the one?" and "How important is physical attraction?" and even, "Should we be dating at all, or should we be courting?" (What do any of these words even mean?) There are worries about being able to afford a wedding, being ready for kids, figuring out gender roles (what does the Church really say about mothers working outside the home?), and so much more.

There's division in the Church over liturgies and rites and even interpretations of certain doctrines: for instance, is using Natural Family Planning to avoid pregnancy acceptable only in very grave circumstances, or as normal practice, or is it even okay at all? Do we need to restrict ourselves to dating people who already agree with us on all these things? And for that matter, do we even need to restrict ourselves to dating only Catholics? I know some very devout Catholic women who ended up dating or marrying Protestant men, possibly because they just got tired of the awkwardness and lack of initiative they encountered among Catholic men and decided "Catholic" wasn't the top criterion on their list anymore.

I also know some Catholics who seem to make "Catholic" practically their only criterion, being willing to date any Catholic who will have them and "make it work." Is this the right approach? In this time when it's so hard to find an attractive, funny, intelligent, devout Catholic spouse, should we all just lower our standards, let go of our preferences, and "make it work"?

This book is an attempt to mostly answer these questions. I say "mostly" because the answer is often, "It depends; use prudence." But your prudence can be informed by guidelines and others' experience, which I've gathered in these pages.

Some of that experience is my own. I'm a Catholic woman, twenty-eight as I finish writing this book, and engaged to be married by the time the book is printed. I've encountered a lot of these questions myself as I dated in college and afterward, and I've spoken to lots of other single Catholics about this topic too. I've also interviewed experts—psychologists, matchmakers, ministry leaders, and, of course, real couples who went through it all and are finally happily married. I started writing on the Catholic dating culture and decline in marriage rates as a freelance journalist a few years ago, while also running a Catholic singles' ministry. And then I was asked to take my findings and put them together into a book full of practical tips for dating and finding a spouse as a Catholic today.

This is the result. I tried to write the book I wish I had read when I was eighteen and just starting to go out into the dating world. And I hope, whether you're eighteen or closer to forty, whether you've never been on a date or have dated a lot and still find the whole process mystifying, that this book will be helpful to you too.

This book assumes that you are Catholic and devout enough to want to do God's will, are fairly sure you're called to marriage, that you know and agree with the basic Church teachings on marriage and chastity—and that you're in a place where you can hear some difficult truths. To benefit at all from reading this book, you'll have to have a little humility and admit that you might need to do something differently to make marriage happen, but also recognize that there's no one magic formula, because another person (plus God) is involved.

That's both the beauty and the challenge of relationships, isn't it? That two people have to be in the right place at the right time *and* do the right things, all in line with God's will, in order for the relationship to blossom. In addition, they need some standards to judge whether or not they are right for each other, while remaining open to being pleasantly surprised. They need a blend of idealism and realism, action and prayerful discernment. So the title of this book is both a silly pun and a real statement of the book's goal: to help you find someone who's attractive enough (pretty) and with enough character (good) so that you can build a happy, holy marriage. Because there's no perfection in this life, we can't go looking for someone who's already a saint and a fashion model; we have to let go of perfectionism, but retain realistic standards. Hence, "pretty good."

I fear this is only a "pretty good" book about how to date and discern marriage. But maybe "pretty good" is actually more practical and relatable than "perfect." That's my hope, anyway.

With that, let's dive in with the first step: meeting people.

1

· · · · · · · · · · ·

You Don't Have a Type

Open Your Mind without Lowering Your Standards

The first step to getting married is meeting someone to marry, right? Not exactly. The first step is meeting lots of people, in hopes that *one* of them will end up being someone you want to marry.

Think of your dating life as a funnel, which starts out broad at the top, but narrows as it goes along. In business, salespeople talk about their "funnels": lots of people hear about the business, only a subset of those people are interested in purchasing the product, and even fewer end up actually choosing to buy. Similarly, you need to meet lots of people who may or may not be a good fit for you before you can start to discern whom you want to choose as a spouse.

In college, my campus chaplain started off a talk for the female students by saying, "If you're like most women, you probably have *the list*." My friends and I glanced at each other with guilty, suppressed laughter: whether in late-night conversations or our diaries, we all had lists of the traits we were looking for in a spouse. Most marriage-minded Catholics—and non-Catholics too, of course—set off on their dating journeys armed with this list of ideal traits. You probably already know that your list of qualities shouldn't contain too many shallow preferences or be too focused on appearance. But you have probably been advised to "know what you're looking for" and "have high standards," and so you've interpreted that to mean you need a list (whether written or mental).

I'm going to advise a completely different approach. I'm going to advise you to get rid of your list—or at least, set it aside for now. Instead of treating it as an inscription in stone, treat it as, at best, a very rough draft on a napkin. Why? Because no one who is single knows for sure what sort of spouse would make them happiest and holiest. Too often, our lists are based on our own fantasies or on fiction, not on real people.

For example, my physical "type" for many years looked suspiciously like Jimmy Stewart's character from *It's a Wonderful Life* (my childhood celebrity crush). As I started dating, I tended to gravitate toward stoic, introverted men who reminded me of myself and a lot of the men in my family. Nothing is necessarily wrong with these traits, but after a lot of trial and error, I learned I actually do better with someone who's different than I am, rather than similar . . . and I can be very attracted to a totally different physical type, too.

How did I learn all this? By challenging myself to be more open to whomever God put in my path. Instead of starting with a list of criteria in priority order and comparing it to the men I met, I adopted two guiding principles. The first I call "just meet people," and the second I call "default to yes."

Just Meet People

Again, the first step is to fill the top of your "funnel" by meeting lots of people, particularly single people of the opposite sex. Beyond that, you shouldn't start off with many filters.

Before writing this book, I founded a local Catholic singles' initiative. For one event, we had a cocktail hour and invited Cristina Pineda, a professional matchmaker and dating coach who is also a devout Catholic, to give us dating tips. She started off by emphasizing how important it is to meet new people regularly, getting outside your typical sphere: "Your social life is a bubble, and you and your future spouse are in two different bubbles that need to come together," said Pineda.

Dr. Henry Cloud, a Christian psychologist, takes this a step further by making it a challenge. In his excellent book *How to Get a Date Worth Keeping*, Cloud challenges his readers to meet *five* new "eligibles"— single people of the opposite sex—per week. He issued the challenge first to a woman (whom he calls Lillie), and he told her to meet five single men, have enough of an interaction with each that they would want to go out with her, *and* make sure they have enough information to follow through on that desire. In other words, they needed to chat with her long enough to be at least mildly interested and end up with her phone number (or at least her full name so they could look her up on social media, I suppose).

Although Lillie was aghast at first and thought the assignment was impossible, Cloud explains that the assignment wasn't to get five good dates a week, but to practice interacting with men in a way that would eventually attract the right ones: "She thought she had to find five men she would be interested in. To her, this meant that they had to have certain requirements. . . . [But] the assignment was not about finding a man, but about finding *herself*. She had lost access to that part of herself that has to do with men and women connecting," says Cloud.

In other words, set aside your list of requirements and *just meet people*. Tap into your ability to chat with strangers, especially of the opposite sex, and be warm, friendly, and open, so that people will want to spend time with you and maybe even go on a date. Consider challenging yourself to meet five a week, or, if that seems too intimidating, at least *one*. Of course, it's a great idea to prioritize filling the top of your funnel with lots of Catholics, but there's no need for everyone you meet to be Catholic or even Christian at this stage. You're just meeting people. There's very little risk in just meeting people, as long as you're meeting them in safe public places.

It might sound silly, but I remember declining to go to a Catholic event at a parish I didn't normally attend because I didn't think my "type" of Catholic guys would be there—meaning that the guys I thought I would meet there were probably not the same "flavor" of Catholicism as I am. Now I laugh at myself for being such a snob. Firstly, if

I went, what would stop a guy of my "tribe" from coming too? Secondly, how could I know for sure that God didn't want me to meet someone of a different "tribe" and bring some good out of that? And thirdly, what could be the harm in just meeting people, anyway?

When I looked deep, I realized I had an illogical fear that I would . . . what? Accidentally marry someone I didn't want to marry? Whatever the thing is that you're not doing because you say, "I don't think I'd want to date the people there," give it a try, just to meet people. Have a friend go with you and hold you accountable to meeting at least one new person of the opposite sex. Even if you're proven correct and you're not interested in anyone there, you're no worse off. Even if it's incredibly awkward, you might have a funny story to laugh about with your friend later. But if you never try, you won't know.

As someone I met at a Young Catholic Professionals conference put it, "Dating is just networking." It's true: both getting a spouse and getting a job begin with expanding how many new people you're meeting and seeing what happens from there. A new connection is nearly always a good thing, and a unique person—an image of God, whether Catholic or attractive or not—is always worth encountering. It never hurts to meet people.

Default to Yes

This principle sounds a little cryptic, but at its core, it's an encouragement to go on at least one date with anyone, and then continue going on one more date, until and unless there's a good reason not to. It's also an encouragement to remain open to conversations, exchanging contact information, and everything else that could lead to a date—until and unless there's a good reason not to.

Dr. Cloud has a whole chapter titled "Go Out with Almost Anyone Once, and Maybe Again." The title says it all: give anyone a chance, unless he or she is dangerous in some way . . . and even if the first date isn't that great, consider giving him or her a second chance. First date jitters and all kinds of other factors can get in the way of making a great first impression. Many happy marriages have come from lackluster first dates, according to experts like Cloud and Pineda and many ordinary couples too.

The "default to yes" principle goes for men and women, though the practical ways of implementing it are a little different.

For women

If a man asks you out, and you don't have any reason to think he's a threat to your morals or safety, and you're not absolutely repulsed by him, say yes! Then, if the date is good or even a little "meh," but he asks you out again, say yes again.

Pineda, who co-founded the firm Matchmakers in the City and has heard date feedback from hundreds of male and female clients, told me that a woman's attraction to a man often develops over time. For this reason, she recommends giving a man at least three dates before deciding you're not attracted to him, romantically or physically. In fact, you should go on dates "until you hit the SRS: Sudden Repulsion Syndrome," says Pineda, "where you would rather be curled up on a beanbag chair in your house than go on a date with this person."

I found her advice on this to be true in my own life. When I first met my fiancé, Enrique, I didn't feel attracted to him or interested at all. He just didn't look like my physical "type" or sound like someone I'd want as a boyfriend. After we met a few more times, I thought he seemed like a really good guy, but I still didn't *feel* anything special for him. But when we both attended a speed dating event, I decided to give him a chance, and another, and another. With each date, I could see more of his good qualities and things we had in common, so my interest grew. And after our third date, I realized that I actually really, *really* liked him.

With other guys, it was pretty similar: by date two or three, I was usually either all-in, or I was "getting the ick," as they say. I was always glad that I had gone on two or three dates, rather than one or zero, because I could be much more confident in my decision. Sometimes, going on two or three dates also allowed the guy to see for himself that we weren't a great fit, so that the ending could be a little more mutual and friendly.

So often, we women decline to give a man a chance out of fear of "leading him on." It's good to be concerned for the other's feelings and try to treat men fairly, of course. But I think we often use this as an excuse when really, we're just afraid of the vulnerability and risk of hurt feelings inherent in dating. We become so afraid of giving the wrong impression that we shut a man down without giving him a fair shot. At our singles' event, Pineda made a helpful point: "As long as there's still a question mark, you're not leading him on." The whole point of dates, she explained, is to get to know someone better and see whether your interest grows or wanes.

If it's helpful, I've also heard from a number of great guys that they wish Catholic women would say yes more. They don't seem to feel led on if a woman says yes to a few dates and then decides to end it, because they can understand that she gave them real consideration and then declined. What bothers them much more is being dismissed after or even before a first date, before they really have a chance to shine. So, if a guy asks you out a second or third time, and you're thinking "maybe," default to yes!

This is all especially true if he's a practicing Catholic. It might be a good idea to accept at least one date with a non-Catholic Christian or other morally upright person (more to come in the chapter on dating non-Catholics). But if you're dealing with a man who's Catholic, actually goes to Mass on Sundays, and seems to believe Church teaching, you've already found a relatively rare diamond in the rough! Keep giving him a chance for as long as your interest in him is growing, even a little.

By the way, it's possible to say no to a man with your body language and tone before he ever asks you out. Default to yes here too. Instead of sticking close to your female friends and your phone when you're out, make a conscious effort to make eye contact and smile (even across the room). When you're in a conversation with a man, ask questions and give answers that keep the conversation flowing, unless you have a good reason not to. And if you already think you *are* interested, amp the same efforts up to eleven.

Some women feel shy about this, as if they're being too forward, but I have heard from countless men that they wish women were *more* overt when displaying their interest. In the introduction, I mentioned my male friend's frustration with women "smiling and moving their hair," whether they're interested or not. Enrique also told me he waited until the speed dating event to ask me out because, before that, he never saw any hint of interest from me. "You gotta give me *something*," he explained later. If we want men to pursue us, we need to show that we're willing to be pursued, and that means at least acting *friendly* to everyone we meet. Then, we need to act a little more obvious and even flirtatious (in an appropriate way) to those we particularly want to pursue us.

One final word: "default to yes" also means "don't default to putting men in the friendzone"! I know several women who have "friendzoned" men when they first met (using either direct or indirect language to let them know this clearly) only to fall head-over-heels for them later. Getting to know the man's personality more deeply, even by hanging out "as friends" rather than explicitly going on dates, caused them to become attracted to him. Sometimes, the men reciprocated, but often they didn't (which was probably why they were willing to be just friends to begin with).

Let's face it: men and women are naturally supposed to find each other attractive, and proximity tends to encourage that. Wouldn't it be much better to be open to the possibility of a date from the start, rather than pretending that this male-female reality isn't there? Especially if it means running up against it later, at a more awkward stage? Ladies, whenever you meet someone that you like well enough to see as a friend, keep the door to romance at least partly open. Default to yes . . . or at least to "maybe"!

Side note: should women pursue?

While we're at it, should men always be the pursuers? The short answer is yes. First of all, every man and nearly every woman I've ever met prefers that the men make the first obvious move, so why not go with that? Secondly, countless matchmakers and other experts agree that this is just what works. Biologically, the sex that incurs the most risk in reproduction (pregnancy and breastfeeding) is wired to be more cautious and selective when it comes to potential mates, so the other needs to pursue and prove himself worthy.

Ladies, if you have made the first move before, please don't feel guilty or ashamed! It's not a sin—it's just not likely to be the most successful strategy long-term. I've seen female friends try to pursue men they're interested in by directly asking them out or simply stating, "I like you," and while I genuinely admire their bravery, the men never stuck around for long. If they are handed an opportunity to have a relationship with a lovely woman, they sometimes go along with it, but they tend to remain passive in the relationship. This passivity is dissatisfying for them (men generally enjoy a challenge, in my experience) and dissatisfying for the woman in the end (we *want* to be pursued and feel desired, don't we?).

There will be exceptions to everything, of course, so there are probably plenty of happy couples out there who started off with the woman making the first move. But the general rule stands: a man who is interested and ready *will* pursue, so a woman is more likely to end up with a man who's truly interested in her if she doesn't do the pursuing.

But again, that doesn't mean that women are purely passive throughout. Especially in an initial conversation, a woman does need to encourage next steps. Pineda gave me some examples of things a woman can say to show interest without becoming the pursuer: "If they're talking about basketball, it's fine for the woman to say, 'I'd love to go to a game someday.' If they're talking about boats, 'Oh, that river sounds amazing.'" In other words, call attention to the fact that you'd be open to doing something fun with him in the future, then let him take the lead from there, rather than directly asking him out or handing him your number.

For men

As the ones who generally pursue women, your "default to yes" is a little different. It does not mean that you should ask out every woman you meet. But it means that every time a single woman catches your attention, you should default to introducing yourself and having a conversation. If the conversation is enjoyable enough that you would like to talk with her more, default to asking her out.

Men are sometimes concerned about being too forward or leading a woman on whom they might not be interested in later. But again, this fear could be holding you back from what might be a great relationship and even a marriage! When you notice a woman who sparks your interest, the first step is just to introduce yourself in a friendly way and chat as you would with any acquaintance.

If you ask her out immediately, she might panic and default to no: women are biologically wired to avoid risk, so they need to feel comfortable around someone before taking the step even to a first date. I can speak from experience here; someone asked me out once within about twenty seconds of introducing himself. I was impressed—so much so that it *did* ultimately lead to us dating for a while—but in the moment, I panicked and exited the conversation as quickly as I could. At least five minutes of small talk would have helped a lot.

But don't drag it out too long. Cristina Pineda recommends talking with a woman for no more than ten minutes before either asking for her number or politely exiting the conversation (e.g., "It was great to meet you. I'm going to grab another drink. Have a nice night!"). That way, you're not leading her on (a lengthy conversation will give her the impression that you're very interested in her) or monopolizing her time if there's some other guy who wants to meet her. While ten minutes is a good rule of thumb, you shouldn't be continually glancing at the time, of course; just have a conversation, and if you're really enjoying it enough to continue for ten minutes or more, that's a great sign that you should ask her out!

How exactly should you do that? There are plenty of ways to phrase it, starting with the very direct, "Will you go on a date with me?" This might work if your conversation has been going very, *very* well and she's clearly interested. But the word "date" has come to sound very serious among a lot of Catholics (who tend to think that you need to be exclusive and actively considering marriage right away if you're dating), so it's not always the best approach. I recommend saying something like, "I don't want to take up all your time tonight, but I have really enjoyed our conversation. I'd love to continue it over dinner sometime. Could I get your number?" This puts you clearly in the position of the pursuer and implies you're going to take her out in a possibly-romantic way, but also makes it clear that your aim for now is just to continue the conversation and continue getting to know her— it's not too high-pressure. (More on exclusivity and types of dates in the upcoming chapters.)

Now, most men believe they have a type just like women do, only more so. In my experience, there is some truth to the stereotype that men tend to care more about specific hair or eye colors, body types, and other physical attributes than most women do (or at least, than most women will admit). And I know men, including my wonderful fiancé, who say that they just don't find women with a particular hair color attractive enough to pursue. I respect that, and I won't suggest that you force yourself to ask out women you aren't interested in. But I will share some examples of men who set aside their physical criteria, with good results.

First, another example from Pineda. As a guest on Relevant Radio's "Trending with Timmerie," she shared the story of a male client who found success outside his normal type. "He only wanted to date short brunettes," she shares. But when nothing worked out, the matchmakers finally asked him to go out with a tall, blonde woman, "and they hit it off, and they are now married," said Pineda. So, gentlemen, if someone offers to set you up with a woman who isn't your physical type, but has deeper traits you want, give it a shot! Or, if you meet a woman at an event and end up in a pleasant conversation, be open to the idea of taking her out at least once and seeing how you feel after spending a little more time with her. A date doesn't mean you have to marry her.

If you have a female friend who shares important values and goals with you, be open to considering her as a dating prospect, too. Catholic writer Emily Stimpson Chapman has shared on Instagram and elsewhere that her husband spent ten years in an ambiguous "datey friendship" with her before realizing that he should marry her. Now, Chapman herself points out that this is very rare, and that most women shouldn't *let* a man hang around for ten years without making a move. But in their case, it worked out: he had to let go of his desire for "instant fireworks," and he discovered that their friendship was an excellent foundation for love.

If you enjoy your female friend's company so much, what exactly is it that makes you think you would never marry her? Is it an item on your list of "wife criteria" that's actually too limiting, and possibly not that important after all? On the other hand, if you really won't marry her, is it charitable to keep hanging around and possibly warding off other men, maybe even causing her to develop feelings for you that you won't reciprocate? Give her a chance, at least in your mind, and then set up a respectful boundary if you are not going to pursue her romantically.

One last note for men. I know that rejection is extraordinarily painful. As the pursuers, you tend to bear the brunt of hearing "no" more often. On behalf of all women, thank you for bearing that load and for taking risks anyway. Please don't let fear of rejection hold you back, even if you've heard "no" a lot. Ultimately, it only takes one "yes" to change your life, and then every no will be worth it.

Besides, in a frustrating paradox, women tend to find a man more attractive if he exudes confidence and takes the lead. A man who shows his interest clearly, asks for her number, calls quickly to ask her out, puts thought into making it a fun date, and *maybe* even tries (*very* gently and respectfully) a second time if she initially shuts him down— that's a man who is showing that he's ambitious and willing to put in effort. And those are very attractive qualities. Say a prayer, take a deep breath, and ask her out. If you don't, you might regret it forever!

Working together to build a new dating culture

Ultimately, these principles—"just meet people" and "default to yes"—work best when we all work together. If people refuse to go somewhere because "no good guys/girls go there," the statement will remain true. But if everyone goes more places with an eye to meeting new people, meeting new people will become easier. If men default to pursuing all the women who catch their attention, and women default to saying yes (or at least maybe) to men who pursue them, everyone would go on more dates. Remember, dating is just networking! If everyone builds a "just meet people" habit, everyone will have more prospects in the top of their funnels, giving everyone a higher chance of finding a spouse. It's a cultural shift that needs to happen, especially in Catholic circles.

But shouldn't you still have some standards and not just date everybody? Yes, but relationships happen in stages; meeting someone and going on a first date (or even a second or fifth) is very far from marriage. We'll talk more in Chapter Four about the stages of a relationship. First, we'll talk more about exactly how and where to "just meet people" so that you have a chance to "default to yes."

2

. . . .

Online Meeting, Not Online Dating

Five Principles for Getting Offline as Quickly as Possible

It's a polarizing topic, online dating. On one hand, people complain about sending dozens of messages just to get one response, or receiving dozens of messages that just say "Hi." People end up with texting pen-pals but no real dates, or get ghosted altogether. Two women have told me that men they met online canceled their dates at the last minute because they were either drunk or hungover—not a good look!

On the other hand, lots of people do, in fact, meet a great Catholic spouse on the Internet. Nowadays, online dating is too important to be ignored.

Full disclosure: I never tried online dating myself. I was always against it; it sounded like the worst aspects of a job application, high school dance, and shopping on Amazon all rolled into one. I preferred to max out in-person opportunities, matchmakers, and pretty much anything else before I'd resort to that, and I encouraged my friends and siblings to stay away, too.

But doing the research for this book actually caused me to come around. Luckily, as I write this, I'm engaged to a wonderful man I met in person, but if I were still single, knowing what I know now, I'd probably try a dating site or two alongside my in-person efforts. The fact is that online dating is just like most things: there are better and worse ways to do it. It takes some effort to do it well, but the reward can be great.

I talked to employees at some of the top Catholic dating sites as well as several real-life Catholic couples who met on secular dating sites, and I distilled their wisdom into general advice that can be used on almost any dating site, even as the features change. Here are five principles for online dating that will help you meet the right people and actually go on some great dates.

Five Principles for Online Meeting

1. Meet in person as soon as possible

The first principle of good online dating is that the dating part doesn't really happen online.

In his video "7 Rules for Successful Online Dating," Catholic psychologist Greg Bottaro (who met his wife online) calls the phrase "online dating" a misnomer: he prefers the term "online meeting," because the real dating—that is, getting to know someone—happens in person. Bottaro recommends keeping email and texting to a minimum before moving to a phone call, and scheduling a real, in-person date after no more than a week of talking. "Being in the room with somebody, hearing somebody's voice, seeing their facial expressions—these are all really important parts of seeing who somebody is," says Bottaro. (Of course, distance might make it impossible to meet within a week; more on what to do instead a little later.)

Go easy on the texting

The danger with lots of text-based communication is that people tend to present themselves differently in writing and online than they do in person. It's easy to get very emotionally attached to the other person—but only based on what he or she has chosen to tell you in a carefully crafted message. You are likely to see only a highly curated, filtered version of your love interest's personality this way.

My friend Kayla (who met her husband on OkCupid) told me she decided to meet each of her matches in person as quickly as possible, after messaging enough to determine he wasn't a "complete lunatic." (Of course, she met them in public places for safety, too.) "There's only so much you can do over a screen, but being in the same room with a person, you get so much more spoken and unspoken communication," said Kayla.

Her instinct is well-founded. Some people are deliberately dishonest about who they are, to the point of catfishing: faking an entire identity online in order to lure someone into a relationship. In a 2016 blog post, Catholic writer Chase Padusniak rather famously shared his story of being catfished: he had "dated" a woman he met on Twitter for months before eventually finding out she was not who she said she was . . . and that she was already married. Others are not deliberately dishonest, but in an effort to put their best foot forward, they accidentally portray themselves inaccurately or incompletely.

Even if both people portray themselves accurately, that extra nonverbal communication can change whether or not you are attracted to someone in person. I experienced something like this going into my freshman year of college. The college administration created a Facebook group for incoming freshmen so we could get to know each other and make connections before showing up on campus. I connected with a young man I'll call Calvin and quickly wound up exchanging messages with him almost daily. I didn't necessarily think of him as a dating prospect, but it was nice to have a connection with someone from my class. We progressed from small talk to somewhat deeper things— nothing too intimate, but things that one usually doesn't share right away with a new acquaintance in person. I was a shy teenager, but also a born writer, and typing out long messages to Calvin was an easy way to feed my desire for friendship and connection.

And then we showed up on campus. In real life, poor Calvin and I could barely hold a conversation. Neither of us had intentionally misrepresented ourselves, but we were both a lot shyer in person than we were online. He had also developed a crush on me that I couldn't re-quite—on my end, there just wasn't any chemistry, romantic or other-wise. It was a highly awkward, yet completely avoidable situation. So, keep texting to a minimum before meeting in real life.

Video is second-best

Of course, there might be times you truly can't meet up with some-one within a week due to distance or other circumstances. In that case, at least schedule a video call. Video calls are better than text-based communication (or even phone calls) because they give you a person's facial expressions and some of their body language. And you can know someone a bit better by hearing what they say off the cuff than you can by reading messages. A video chat can also reduce the risk that someone is completely faking a persona. In his blog post, Padusniak expresses regret that he didn't ask for a video call with the married woman from Twitter early on. The technology of video calls is a huge blessing, and using it early and often is a very smart move.

But this is still an incomplete experience. As a friend of mine once said, "There's a difference between communication and a relation-ship." People are more than just their thoughts and words. We need to experience a person's physical presence in order to fully know them. Our faith teaches this, too: as the Gospel of John puts it, "The Word be-came Flesh and dwelt among us." Why did He become flesh? And why does Jesus want us to receive Him physically in the Eucharist? So that we can really get to know Him!

I'll address this further in the chapter on long-distance dating. But for now, keep this in mind: the Internet is a good way to learn that someone exists, but dating starts when you meet in real life.

2. Be as open as possible

This principle is essentially the same as "default to yes" from the previous chapter, but it is particularly applicable to online dating. Online, it's easy to set precise filters and extremely easy to reject peo-ple: you can swipe left, click no, hide, or ignore, without having to see someone's disappointed face. Challenge yourself to be as open as pos-sible, looking for concrete reasons to rule someone out rather than to rule someone in. Mariette Rintoul, Community Experience Manager at CatholicMatch (who also met her own husband on the site) told me, "The most successful people are people who are really, truly open to God's will and allow God to surprise them a little bit."

She shared that a lot of the people who don't meet someone on CatholicMatch and give up quickly are restricting themselves to very specific distances (e.g., 50 miles or less) or very specific age ranges (e.g., within three or five years of their own age). Her own husband is seven and a half years older than herself and lived 1500 miles away when they connected on the site. She had to drop some of her restrictions in order to find someone who matched her desires in more important ways.

"It's that real openness . . . which I think comes down to really seeing the other people on there not as an object you design in your head, but real people with souls," said Rintoul. She also mentioned that CatholicMatch has actually removed some of their filter options over the years, particularly physical traits that truly don't matter in a relationship, like eye color, to discourage users from objectifying people.

Similarly, Dr. Bottaro's first rule for successful online dating is, "You are not looking for 'the One.' You are looking to filter out the 'No's.'" He recommends responding to every like, match, message, wink, or what-have-you for the first two months online. If this sounds crazy, remember the Golden Rule: if you would like to receive more replies when you contact people online, reply to others. After all, if you talk a little bit and discover a real dealbreaker, you can always end the conversation. Have the charity and good manners to at least speak to someone until you have a good reason not to.

My friends Kayla and Rudy are an example of a very healthy level of openness that led to a happy marriage. When Rudy first sent Kayla a message on OkCupid, he pointed out that they were a 97% match, according to the site's question-and-answer based matching process. He also asked her what "super Catholic" meant in her bio. Rudy wasn't Catholic (I guess that was the 3% that didn't match?), but he was interested in learning more about Catholicism. Kayla was open to getting to know him and seeing whether he was heading toward the Catholic Church. He was: Rudy became Catholic before proposing to Kayla.

Their honest, open conversations during their relationship helped Rudy take the plunge across the Tiber, and now they are rearing two beautiful young children in the Catholic Faith.

Aside from the faith difference, they were both open to dating with a height difference: Rudy is five feet, five inches, and Kayla is five feet, seven inches. The stereotype (which has at least some truth to it) is that women on dating apps won't even give the time of day to a man who's shorter than they would like, but Kayla told me it never bothered her at all to be slightly taller than Rudy: "When we first met . . . if I wore something with a little heel, it just took a little getting used to, but that's it," said Kayla. "Honestly, I don't know why I would feel bad or embarrassed about it. It just doesn't make sense." Rudy concurred. When I asked him if men care whether the women they date are taller than themselves, he said, "I think the insecure ones do. . . . I didn't care at all."

In short, ladies and gentlemen, don't filter people by height or any other physical trait when dating online. You could be missing out on an amazing person who not only has good character and compatible life goals, but to whom you could be genuinely attracted as well.

3. Fill Out Your Profile Well

This is probably the most common piece of advice you'll hear about online dating, but it still needs to be said: fill out your profile well. Put your best foot forward while being genuinely yourself.

Photos

Rintoul told me that one of the most important factors for success on CatholicMatch is having multiple good photos. Ask a friend to take photos (not selfies) of you in different settings so that photos not only show what you look like, but also work as conversation-starters. Rintoul's now-husband noticed that one of her photos was taken at her parish, and, although he lived in a different state, he recognized the church as one he had been to when he was visiting a friend. This gave him an "in" to send her a message. Similarly, Amanda, who met her fiancé Chris on Hinge, said she found his profile appealing because his photos presented a full picture of who he was.

On the other hand, there's no need to look excessively polished or professional: Chris mentioned that Amanda's photos drew him in because they looked real and gave the impression that Amanda wasn't superficial or overly focused on her appearance. Amanda also said that it's good to have some photos with friends, "so you're not perceived as a loner type," but your profile should make it very clear which one you are. In short, photos should be clear enough to show what you look like, and they should serve as a way to portray different aspects of your life that someone else might find interesting.

Faith *and* Fun

Of course, your profile should show that you're Catholic. If you're reading this book, it must be at least somewhat important to you to practice your faith and find someone else who shares it, or at least supports it. (More on dating non-Catholics in a later chapter.) So, as part of showing who you are, you should showcase that faith and its importance on your profile. Remember Kayla saying she was "super Catholic"? This was an accurate representation of herself, a great conversation starter, and appealing to the type of man she wanted to attract, particularly on a non-Catholic dating app. Amanda, similarly, had mentioned being Catholic several times throughout her profile in various ways, rather than just in the religion section, to show that it was genuinely important to her.

At the same time, your profile should showcase more than just your faith. Catholics sometimes have the temptation to make themselves appear extremely devout and knowledgeable about obscure Church documents or devotions, but forget that God created fun, too. For examples of what not to do, there's an Instagram account called "Catholic Dating Nightmares" that posts anonymized screenshots of messages, bios, etc. that real Catholics have encountered on dating sites. One post shows someone's introduction, which simply says, "It is hard to talk about yourself when thinking about Christ's sacrifice for me on the cross." It's wonderful if you're meditating that intensely . . . but think about whom you would want to go on a date with: someone who meditates on Christ's Passion, or someone who meditates on Christ's Passion and *also* likes rock climbing?

Remember your audience

As you fill your profile, make sure you include things that could start a conversation with someone of the opposite sex. Amanda and Chris both encountered many profiles they felt were difficult to connect with because they fell too much into generic stereotypes: "80% of girl profiles are like, 'I love to travel, here's my dog, here's me standing in the sunset.' And 80% of guy profiles are blurry bar photos where you can't tell which guy he is, and then, like, fishing," said Amanda. To bridge the gap, Amanda decided to mention a specific podcast she enjoyed and knew that many men would enjoy as well. This proved to be a good conversation starter for Chris.

Again, there's nothing wrong with mentioning travel, fishing, or pets somewhere on your profile if you truly like those things. But showcase as many as possible of your different interests to increase the chances that someone else overlaps with at least one of them. And try getting more specific like Amanda did. Instead of, "I love reading," mention a particular book you just finished and feel like discussing with someone.

A final note: your profile or bio is not the place to simply write a laundry list of what you are looking for in someone else (which comes across as arrogant and about as romantic as a job description). It's also not a place to air your family drama or worst flaws. Just showcase different aspects of your fun, unique self. And if you can't think of anything fun and interesting to put on your profile, that might signal that you need to work on rounding out your life and trying new things!

4. Use the app, but not too much

When I spoke to Chuck Gallucci, founder of Catholic Chemistry, he mentioned that their app is programmed to show people higher in search results if they are active on the site, engaging with other profiles and sending messages frequently. Similarly, Mariette Rintoul told me CatholicMatch will hide profiles from search results if the person hasn't logged in for a long time. So, just as you can't ghost your in-person friend group and then be upset when no one asks you to hang out, you can't ignore your dating app and then be upset when you don't get any dates.

On the other hand, it can become extremely unhealthy to scan profiles or refresh notifications for hours every day. There are lots of reasons for this. My friend Rudy, who used dating apps off and on for several years, shared some of them.

First, it can get discouraging. If you're not getting much attention on the app, or if you keep seeing profiles of people you feel won't be interested in you, it can damage your self-esteem and confidence pretty quickly. You might think you're not affected by the comparison trap, but the sneaky thing about harmful thoughts is that they masquerade as objective truth.

I once encountered someone on the Catholic Dating subreddit who was desperately bemoaning the fact that he hadn't found a mate, and he believed a major reason for that was his height. He was becoming angry with God for making him "so short" and feeling ready to give up on ever finding a wife (at the fresh age of 25). When someone in the comments finally asked him how tall he was, he said he was five feet, eight inches—that is, barely on the shorter side of average for a male, and several inches taller than the average female! Not only was his comparison of himself to others causing him to become fixated on a physical trait that is ultimately unimportant (as mentioned previously), he wasn't even comparing himself very accurately. If you find yourself feeling hopeless or desperate, fixating on perfectly normal aspects of yourself, or even becoming distanced from God, it might be time to take a break from online dating.

Second, too much time on dating apps can lead to a "shopping" mindset. In my interviews for this chapter, I was amazed at how many times the word "shopping" was used to describe the experience of online dating. Rudy told me that, at first, online dating is exciting: "Hey, here's all these people here for me to choose from . . . I can just shop, for lack of a better word." But if he was shopping for women, women were also shopping for him: "You start to feel like you're kind of selling yourself," said Rudy. He found himself tweaking his profile if he didn't get enough attention, hiding things like his career (which he's passionate about), because he feared women wouldn't like it. "I think for someone who's not 100% confident in himself or herself, it does create a problem, because you're constantly thinking, 'How can I get more attention from the opposite sex through this dating app?'" said Rudy.

Third, it's well-known from studies on social media that excessive notifications and internet use in general can lead to a kind of addiction. If there are infinite profiles out there to swipe on or scroll through, it's easy to just . . . keep swiping or scrolling infinitely. However, this can start to take away time from other areas of your life that are ultimately more fruitful. It's important to keep your life in order. Prioritize prayer, work, real-life friendships and social opportunities, and healthy sleep, eating, and exercise habits. Then, use dating apps as just one more way you're trying to meet more people. If it isn't getting you any dates this week, no worries—you have your kickball league, your book club, and an old friend from college to call anyway, and maybe next week someone new will join the site.

Dr. Bottaro recommends spending no more than 30 minutes on your dating site per day to help keep this piece of your life in right proportion to everything else. Whether or not 30 minutes is the right amount of time for you (you might need less or more depending on the site you're using and your other duties in life), choose a time limit and stick to it.

5. Choose your site wisely

Technology changes quickly. By the time this book comes out, there will probably be new dating apps and sites I've never heard of, and the ones I mention in this chapter might have changed their features or even shut down. But when you embark on an online dating journey, here are some things to look for to choose the best dating app for a Catholic who's looking for a holy, happy marriage.

Numbers

Try to find out how large the user base is, whether it's growing, shrinking, or staying about the same, and what the approximate male/female ratio is. (Most secular dating apps have far more men than women, while Rintoul told me CatholicMatch has always had a roughly equal number of each.)

Faith-related features

Look for either a Catholic dating site/app, or a non-Catholic one that allows you to filter by religion. The principle "be as open as possible" is not meant to make you get too involved with people whose religion and values are misaligned with yours. You can consider filtering for Catholics specifically or for Christians in general, based on Kayla and Rudy's example above and the upcoming chapter on dating non-Catholics. Also, look for a site or app that requires more information than just a photo or two and a tiny bio, so that faith and values have a chance to shine through.

Intentional matching features

Stay away from apps like Tinder that show you one bare-bones profile at a time and ask you to accept or reject the person before moving on. These tend to be very objectifying and, because they are so easy to set up and use, they attract a lot of people looking for quick hookups. Look for a site that takes some effort to set up and uses something to help people match with other people based on more important things than looks. Some use a questionnaire to match people with similar answers, while others provide extensive profiles and search capabilities to allow you to match yourself with people who share interests or values. (Just be careful, once again, not to become too picky, and stay open to God's surprises.)

Messaging and conversation-starter features

Look for a site/app that doesn't put too many restrictions on whom you can message and that encourages real, personal messages (as opposed to heavily emphasizing swipes, likes, etc.). For instance, Catholic Chemistry allows users to respond to any part of a profile in order to start a conversation and incorporates fun "this or that" questions and other icebreakers to move people from browsing to talking. In-app voice and video calls are also a plus, so you can chat with someone before giving him or her your real phone number (just as you would in real life).

Company purpose and culture

What does the app or site say about itself? If the marketing materials say it's intended for people who want a long-term relationship, or if the founder says his or her goal was to help people find spouses, that's a good sign that other people who want long-term relationships and spouses will be drawn to the site. It also indicates that, as the makers of the app develop new features, those features will be focused on the right goal.

Is There a Downside?

The principle "be as open as possible" extends beyond the precise filters you set once you're on a dating site. It extends to being open to the idea of trying online dating if you, like me, have been avoiding it. People these days almost live on the internet, so it makes sense to go where the people are!

Amanda said she decided to go online because she lived in a small town where in-person opportunities to meet new single Catholics were scarce. She went on Hinge, met Chris within a few days, and was offline again in three weeks. Chris had initially "sworn off" dating apps: he hoped to have the story of meeting his wife be something more personal, at an event or through a hobby. But the COVID-19 lockdowns hit in 2020, and he realized that the internet was the only option left: "I kind of had to suck it up, so to speak." Will he and Amanda ever regret that their story began online, rather than with a real-life "meet cute"? Probably not, because it's the true story of how they found each other.

Kayla lived in a mid-size city with a thriving Catholic young adult community; still, she kept running into the same people over and over. Nothing romantic had happened yet, so nothing was going to. She went online and met Rudy within a few weeks. Rudy, it turned out, lived within a few miles of her and had probably passed her on the street, but they never would have thought to speak to each other if it weren't for OkCupid.

This is not to say that absolutely everyone has to try online dating. For some people, it might cause more harm than good by triggering addictive patterns or self-defeating thoughts. If you can't control yourself with regard to how much time you're spending scrolling through profiles or tweaking your own bio, maybe you should stay away from the apps for a while.

But almost everyone I speak with about dating, both experts and couples, say that those who are serious about finding a spouse shouldn't dismiss the online options too quickly. Online dating should be one tool in your toolbelt, one of several doors you fling open when you're ready to ask God to bring someone into your life. You never know which one your future spouse is knocking on.

3
. . . .

In-Person Meeting

Putting Yourself Out There,
Beyond Mass and Donuts

Whether or not you use a dating app—and statistics show that you probably do—it's important to meet people in-person as well. Not every great Catholic man or woman is using the dating app you're on, and not everyone shows their best self online. Maybe you long for that real-life "meet-cute" or organic connection, and that's still possible even in the twenty-first century.

In this chapter, I'll share some strategies for meeting eligibles in person, beyond the obvious places like the coffee hour after Mass or young adult Bible study. Most importantly, I'll share the strategies that helped me go from practically never getting dates, to getting almost too many to handle, to eventually getting engaged.

But I'm not the only example. I took a (not quite scientific) poll in a group chat of several hundred local Catholics, asking the married and engaged people how they met their spouses. The top three answers, which were nearly tied, were online, school/university, and Catholic groups/events. Notice that online meeting is not the front-runner; it's on par with two common in-person opportunities. I know many people who met their spouses at church, through friends and family, at parties or wedding receptions, or in unexpected and unusual ways. (One of my housemates told me that her sister and brother-in-law met in the parking lot of a grocery store.)

Of course, to make in-person meeting successful, those social skills and that attitude of openness I mentioned in Chapter One are crucial. If you have the willingness and ability to just meet people, especially single people of the opposite sex, you could meet your spouse anywhere. There's just one catch: you'll probably have to try some things that are a little outside your comfort zone. After all, your comfort zone is full of people you already know and aren't dating.

If you're already going lots of places, even outside your comfort zone, and meeting lots of people, but you still never get any dates, the problem might not be where you go, but *how* you go. So, this chapter will also contain some hard truths about how Catholic women and men perceive each other, and what you can consider doing to make a more attractive first impression. While you shouldn't compromise your values or put on a fake persona to attract the opposite sex, you should make sure to showcase your *best* real self if your goal is to go on dates.

Don't Be Afraid of the "Single" Label

Fresh off my last breakup, I was feeling a bit desperate and wondering how in the world I would meet a good, smart, attractive, marriage-minded Catholic man. I didn't want to go online—I believed I would fall too much into the "shopping" mindset mentioned in the last chapter—so I started looking around for ways to meet single Catholic men who were interested in dating in person. I quickly encountered other local Catholics who were looking for the same thing. There were plenty of ways to meet Catholics here in Nashville, but it was still hard to find ones who were interested in dating and would actually take action. You could have a great connection with someone and then find out that she has a long-distance boyfriend or that he's on the verge of entering seminary.

Or, you could have a great conversation with someone who is similarly single and looking, but never end up on a date because the culture of the event or group subtly discourages dating. There's a vague, unspoken rule that you shouldn't go to Bible study *just* to meet people of the opposite sex; therefore, there's a stigma against asking out someone at Bible study. You're supposed to be there purely out of love for God's Word, don't you know? And if you do ask someone out, and she says no, you definitely can't ask someone else from Bible study too soon, or you'll get a reputation for being *that guy* who asks out all the girls at Bible study.

The result is that men and women tend to congregate in their own groups on opposite sides of the room at every gathering, fearful of appearing too flirtatious by simply speaking to someone of the other sex. (Or, more commonly, they just have separate men's and women's Bible studies.) Socially, it's much safer to express your desire to date in the semi-anonymous forum of an online profile, while in person, acting as if that's practically the furthest thing from your mind.

This subtle stigma against dating is silly, of course. If marriage is a sacrament and a holy state of life, shouldn't Catholic young adult culture encourage finding a spouse, organically, alongside doing other things like studying scripture? But, no matter how silly, the stigma is there, and I wanted to change that. I wanted to create a "safe space" where asking people out and making an effort to meet people of the opposite sex were normal and socially acceptable. So I started a singles' ministry.

Now, the phrase "singles' ministry" still makes me cringe a bit. Somehow, it conjures images of unattractive or socially awkward single people meeting over bad coffee in a church basement. Many people, especially women, have told me that they don't like the idea of going to an event where there's an expectation that everyone is trying to get a date. It feels high-pressure. They're concerned the people there might be too pushy, or just "weird," or that they themselves will feel like failures if they leave without a date. Some men have also told me they wouldn't be interested in this type of event. One young man who messaged me on Reddit said he feared a singles' event might be "90% guys," or even if the ratio were better, that trying to make a good first impression would be "mildly stressful." So if the idea of coming to a Catholic singles' event makes you want to vomit, whether out of disgust or nervousness, I completely understand.

And yet, to my long-lasting astonishment, it *worked*. I started with casual gatherings at a brewery, then progressed to the cocktail hour and talk by Cristina Pineda that I mentioned in Chapter One, then to structured speed dating events. There was nearly always a good turnout, but speed dating in particular was a huge hit, bringing 40-60 people each time and resulting in plenty of first dates. And the types of men and women who showed up were all over the map, from shy or quirky to conventionally attractive social butterflies. Over a seven-month period, we ran three speed dating events that collectively resulted in dozens of dates and at least five long-term relationships, two of which have turned into engagements so far (and those are just the dates and relationships I actually heard about . . . not everyone wants to tell). As of this writing, I have handed off the ministry to a new leader, who's had even more success and is working to get Nashville Catholic Singles recognized as a ministry of the diocese.

What is speed dating?

Speed dating is a way to meet lots of eligible single people all in one evening. Attendees are paired up with each attendee of the opposite sex for a "speed date" that lasts a few minutes. (At my events, we always did seven minutes, so there was time to really get a conversation started.) Attendees then privately indicate (digitally or on paper) which of their "speed dates" they would be interested in going out with. Usually, if people are mutually interested, contact information is exchanged for them by the event hosts or automatically by an app. Invented in the nineties by a Jewish rabbi, speed dating was originally designed to help people meet and marry someone of the same religion, so it translates very well to Catholic dating.

My city (Nashville) isn't the only place that Catholic speed dating is taking off. I recently wrote an article for OSV News about Catholic speed dating ministries around the country, including Hot and Holy in Michigan, AZ Catholic Speed Dating in Arizona, and Denver Catholic Speed Dating in Colorado (which also does pop-up events around the country and even internationally). Could it be that the Holy Spirit is working to revive the Sacrament of Matrimony through *speed dating*, of all things? The founders of these ministries all told me that they were seeing essentially the same issues—lots of single Catholics in the same area, who somehow never date each other, and whose morale has been weakened by the awkwardness of online and long-distance dating. They each had creative ways of making the events successful and fun, and each could point to multiple dates and relationships that had resulted, even though their ministries were very new.

Most singles' ministries also host other events besides speed dating from time to time, such as mixers, game nights, and trivia nights. Dances, which have a long history, are another popular way to meet eligible singles. (Parishes used to host dances for the teenagers and young adults, and for hundreds of years, public balls were an important way for single men and women to meet.) The aforementioned Reddit user who was skeptical of singles' events told me that he and his friends have the most success meeting women at dances organized by a committee of young Catholics. The organizers teach a simple swing or waltz, and people are paired with random partners for the lesson. Afterward, it's expected that the guys will ask the girls to dance, so it feels natural to interact with the opposite sex. "I just find if you're willing to learn how to dance and are easy to talk to, any guy could easily get a date," he said. He also pointed out that, even if the dates don't work out, the dance wasn't a waste of time: "It's fun regardless!"

You may not like dancing, you may find speed dating stressful . . . but you can't possibly know that if you've never tried them! If you're serious about finding a spouse, you really ought to try out purpose-built Catholic singles' events, dances, and anything else that encourages men and women to interact. If you show up with a good attitude and the "just meet people" mindset, these events can be a lot of fun, whether or not you get a date. At a minimum, they help you practice your "just meet people" skills and easily hit your five eligibles per week quota (if you're taking Dr. Cloud's challenge). Plus, Anna Basquez, the founder of Denver Catholic Speed Dating, told me that many of her attendees who didn't meet their spouses at her events still ended up meeting their spouses soon after. There was a kind of ripple effect. Meeting people and getting dates is at least partially a skill that just takes practice.

Of course, the "default to yes" mindset also increases the chances you will get a date at a singles' event. The founders of AZ Catholic Speed Dating told me that they encourage their attendees to "be generous with your yeses" and give people a chance unless there's a good reason not to. I encouraged the same approach at my events, especially for women, who tended to be more selective. If you enjoyed talking for a few minutes, enough that you think you'd like to talk with him for another hour or two, that's probably enough to write his name down. If you're thinking "maybe," it's a yes!

If Catholic speed dating, dances, and mixers don't already happen in your area, try throwing your own event. As Czeena Devera, the founder of Hot and Holy, told me, "You just need a few good friends" to make an event possible. Some events also act as fundraisers (ticket revenue goes to a parish restoration fund or a charity), which might be enough to convince someone who's otherwise skeptical or embarrassed to give it a try ("I'm just donating to a good cause!").

Besides, there's almost nothing bolder and better you can do for your dating life than *lead* the Catholic singles' events. When I was running my Nashville singles' ministry, I got far more dates than I ever had in my life, because everyone knew who I was and had some way of contacting me. (Being asked out via the ministry email might not be very romantic, but it worked.) And it was very rewarding to see my efforts working, both by sparking my relationship with Enrique (more on that later!), and by bringing other people together.

One last thought: ask yourself, if attending an event labeled for singles seems too high-pressure or feels too forward, why doesn't a dating app? Hiding behind a screen might make rejection feel less personal, but it can also make interaction in general feel less personal, hindering the chemistry that would otherwise happen. When a coworker heard about me running a speed dating event, he said, "That sounds like real-life Tinder." He makes a good point: both dating apps and speed dating fulfill the same purpose, filling the top of your funnel with lots of new eligibles. Trying both will help you meet more people, and it will help you meet people in different contexts, so you can learn about what works best for you.

How You Go: Hard Truths about First Impressions

When I interviewed her for this book, matchmaker Cristina Pineda emphasized to me that it's not just about where you go to meet dates, it's *how* you go. You could go all the places in the world and in cyberspace but still not get any dates if your appearance or attitude tends to repel people of the opposite sex. Very often, men and women don't really know what the other sex tends to like, or don't care, and then wonder why they aren't getting any dates (or the type of dates they want).

Now, there's an enormous variety of people out there with vastly different preferences, and there's a lot of truth to the idea that you should just "be yourself." For example, there are a lot of people who prefer to date people who are willing to sleep with them on the third date; be yourself by holding fast to your moral standards! Even in less serious matters, I do *not* recommend putting on a fake persona or hiding your likes and dislikes just to get dates.

But just as we can develop our characters and genuinely become better people, we can also develop our personalities and style of self-presentation to genuinely become more attractive to the kind of people we *want* to attract. There's nothing wrong or fake about this, because it's real self-improvement: becoming more who we really are and want to be. We put effort and money into making a good first impression for things like job interviews all the time, so why not do the same when it comes to meeting men and women we could date?

With that foundation laid, I'll share some things I've learned about what Catholic men and women are often looking for in each other, so that you can take them into consideration. Maybe there are some things that you're just doing out of habit (not because they're important to you) that are keeping you from putting your best foot forward with the opposite sex. Don't change yourself drastically, but be willing to consider some small tweaks.

Personality and interests

Being a woman and hearing from other Catholic women about their dating experiences, I find there's a running theme: Catholic men are often boring. That sounds harsh, but hear me out—or rather, hear out some of the women I've spoken with on the topic. When I wrote an article for OSV News about the decline in Catholic marriages, one woman told me she had tried dating both Catholics and non-Catholics, and the Catholic men were "rather uninteresting." She said, "They didn't seem to have much to talk about. There was no joking or flirting. They tended to have few hobbies and interests, when compared to other men I tried to date."

Other women have told me that it's difficult to find a faithful Catholic man who's committed to chastity and knows Church doctrine, but also knows how to talk about other things besides theology. (There's a married man in my local Catholic community who spotted this trend and started teasing his single friends for being too nerdy about their Catholicism around women: "Don't mention the Fourth Lateran Council on a first date!" he says.)

One could object that it's better to marry someone who's faithful and smart even if he's a little nerdy, than one who's good at flirting and has fun hobbies but lacks depth. This is absolutely true, but isn't it best to have both? When Jesus walked the earth, He must have been a good conversationalist and a pleasant person to be around. He was familiar with the culture around Him and the things that concerned His followers in their daily lives, in addition to preaching salvific wisdom. Why else would He get invited to so many dinner parties and a wedding? And why would so many of His parables and instructions be about everyday things like food, farming, clothes, and money?

Many of the saints were known for their wittiness and senses of humor: St. Teresa of Avila, St. John Bosco, and St. Philip Neri, to name a few. Some of the modern-day saints are well known for their hobbies and social lives, too: Pier Giorgio Frassati was famously into skiing. Catholics should strive for virtue and intellectual depth as well as the other aspects of our God-given humanity that make relating to other people easier and more enjoyable. In the last chapter, I suggested that Catholics should include more than their faith on their dating profiles; in the same way, Catholics should have more to talk about in person.

Here's something to consider too: if your only conversation topics are theological or your only interest is serving at the altar (or some other Catholic devotion), does this stem from scrupulosity or hide some deeper fear? If the idea of playing a sport, taking a swing dancing class, or seeing a clean comedy show seems un-Catholic to you, pray and think about why that might be, and consider speaking with a spiritual director or a wise married person about it. Another person's viewpoint can be very helpful when determining how to be "in the world but not of it." And interests like dancing, sports, and comedy easily turn into date ideas when you find a woman who shares the interest.

Of course, women can be guilty of being boring or scrupulous too, and both sexes can be guilty of the opposite extreme: shallowness and unconcern for the things of God. This is one reason it's important to prioritize our relationship with Jesus, through both the Mass and personal, conversational prayer. We become like the people we spend the most time with, so making Jesus our closest friend and confidant will surely lead us all to a more balanced position, whichever extreme we're likely to fall into. By His grace, everything great and small can be an occasion for holiness and deepening our awareness of His love, even secular things. If we truly wanted to focus our minds completely on obviously religious things with no concern for social interaction, we'd have to give up marriage and join a cloistered religious order. And, come to think of it, even nuns have time for recreation. (I know some contemplative Norbertines who play a *brutal* game of Uno.)

So, have a full, fun, well-rounded life. Here's a tip to help with this. Take a look at your life right now and see whether you're doing at least one thing for each of these areas: spiritual, physical, intellectual, social, and emotional. Here are some examples:

1. **Spiritual**: Are you working on the next step in your prayer life and relationship with God (e.g., 30 minutes of mental prayer every day or adding in a weekday Mass once a week)? Are you aware of a virtue you need to develop and taking concrete steps to work on it?

2. **Physical**: Are you getting sufficient exercise? If not, committing to a daily run or gym workout is great, but consider a form of exercise that could double as a social activity, like a dance class or softball league.

3. **Intellectual**: Interesting people are always learning something new. If you need a refresher on the Catechism or the Bible, joining a good study group or taking an online class might be a good idea. But it's okay and good to study not-so-Catholic things too, like a new language or a new professional skill. Or just pick up a good classic book and commit to reading a bit of it every day. (Personally, I'm a huge reader, but there are times when I've fallen out of my reading habit and into a major social media habit. I found that the quality of my conversations drastically declined when my mind was full of nothing but funny memes, and rapidly improved when I went back to reading good books.)

4. **Emotional**: We all have an emotional need for deep connection, intimacy, and love, and most of us have some emotional wounds from our past life. As you deepen your prayer life, ask the Lord to reveal any emotional wounds or unmet needs you may have and guide you to a solution, whether it be finding a therapist or deepening your relationship with one or two good friends or family members so that you can experience (and practice building) a satisfying emotional intimacy with other people. (While we're at it, Dr. Bob Schuchts's book *Be Healed* is an excellent resource for working on your relationship with Jesus and being healed of emotional wounds all at once.)

5. **Social**: Obviously, if you're going to meet people, you need a social life, and you need practice with how to relate to people as casual acquaintances. Pineda recommends going to at least one social (non-work) event per week, such as a Catholic young adult group, a volunteer opportunity, or a party. Strike a balance between continuing to deepen your relationships with existing friends and gradually expanding your social circle by going places where you'll meet new people.

I like this list because the different aspects can help balance each other out. If you tend to be very introverted or want to stay home a lot, it's good to get out of your comfort zone and stretch the edges of your social sphere. But if you tend to be someone who can hardly stand to be alone, prioritizing your spiritual and emotional life a bit more by going to adoration alone one night a week might be a good idea. Investing in your own spiritual, intellectual, and emotional depth ensures you won't be shallow, and investing in your social and physical life ensures you won't be too cerebral and inwardly-focused and come across as boring.

One more thing: keep some time open to actually go on dates! Keep at least one or two nights a week, or one or two weekends per month, free of commitments and travel plans so that you have time to devote to the right someone who comes along.

Appearance

To women: whether or not you think it's okay for women to pursue men, you probably long for a man to pursue you. There's something both thrilling and profoundly relaxing about receiving a man's attentions and following his lead. While that means that men do more of the work in the beginning of the relationship, we women have to do some work to allow men to see us as available for and worthy of pursuit. I already talked in Chapter One about the "default to yes" principle and making sure your words and body language show openness or interest rather than turning a man away. But now, it's time to talk about appearance.

Both men and women should put some effort into their appearance when going anywhere that eligible single people might be (which, as I've already said, is technically anywhere). For men, good hygiene, a decent haircut, and simple, well-fitting clothes go a long way. For women, those same things go an even longer way, because men typically do not feel interested enough to walk up to a woman and introduce themselves, much less ask her out, if they don't already feel a spark of physical attraction.

What tends to cause that spark? When I took a survey of 300 Catholics asking about their dating journeys, I asked what they found attractive and unattractive in the opposite sex. Men often said that they wanted women who were "feminine." They weren't picky about the details, but they wanted a woman who looked like a woman, different from themselves and therefore fascinating.

Does this mean every woman has to wear dresses all the time, keep her hair long, like pink, giggle, or anything else stereotypically feminine? Not necessarily. I will say that when I've talked with guy friends and brothers about this topic, they pretty consistently say that they love to see women wear skirts and dresses. "It just looks so much nicer," one friend told me. Pineda always recommends that women wear a form-fitting (that is, figure-flattering—it doesn't need to be skintight) dress on a first date. Personally, I've consistently noticed that I get more male attention (particularly the positive, uplifting kind, not the creepy kind) when I'm in a pretty dress, rather than sweatpants. Lots of men do like long hair, too: my fiancé loves to see "fun hair," which means anything braided, curly, or intricate, and he's not alone. These are things you might *consider* incorporating into your appearance, particularly when you are going somewhere eligible Catholic men are. But notice that I say "consider," not "force yourself at all costs." If something just isn't you, it won't attract someone who likes *you*, so it's no good! But it's worth playing with your wardrobe and grooming to find what colors and silhouettes are most attractive on *you*.

If all of this sounds shallow, or you believe that Catholics shouldn't be concerned with fashion or adorning the body, allow me to quote a few saints to you. St. Thomas Aquinas asks in the *Summa Theologica* (question 169, article 2) whether women should adorn themselves, and he concludes that it is not sinful for women to adorn themselves "soberly and moderately" (rather than "excessively, shamelessly, and immodestly"). It would be a problem, he says, for a woman who has chosen a celibate state of life to adorn herself with the purpose of getting men's attention, which is why nuns wear very plain and conservative clothing. But if you don't plan to be a nun, it is fitting to attract men's attention—just not the "wrong kind of attention," as our mothers and grandmothers call it. Similarly, St. Francis de Sales says in the *Introduction to the Devout Life* that, just as a married woman should dress attractively for her husband as part of keeping the relationship happy, an unmarried woman may dress attractively, for "maidens . . . may lawfully desire to attract many, although only with the view of ultimately winning one in holy matrimony."

Side note: *modesty for women* **and** *men*

"Modesty"—that word had to come up eventually in a section on women's appearance! It is unavoidable because modesty is very important for getting dates—from the right men. Once, a young man I know met a girl at a party and hit it off really well. When he saw her again, she was wearing (according to his description to me later) "very, *very* short shorts and a shirt with no sleeves at all," and he just couldn't "deal with it," so he didn't walk over and start another conversation. I imagine she was a wonderful woman who only intended to dress comfortably for the summer, but to this young Catholic man, she looked too unclothed for him to feel comfortable around her. Too often, we women allow the fashion industry to pressure us into wearing less and less, when more breathable fabrics would be just as cool (and would sometimes look more flattering and even reduce body image issues—I used to think my thighs were too big, until I realized that shorts have just gotten too small!).

I promised you hard truths, and I know this is an especially hard one! It's easy for women today to say that men are responsible for their own thoughts, so women shouldn't have to cover up for their sake. Sure, but what if they responsibly choose to control their thoughts by turning away and focusing on someone else? If you work at a store, you signal that you work there by wearing your uniform, so that customers will know they can ask you for help. Similarly, if we want to attract men who are trying to respect women by getting to know them as people and not just focusing on their sex appeal, we signal that by wearing something that doesn't *over*-emphasize our sex appeal, causing it to overshadow everything else.

Modesty is a very, very tricky subject, and I won't go deeper into it here. I will just suggest thinking about what you're wearing and what adjectives you would use to describe it. Good Catholic men will be more attracted to and comfortable around women whose attire can be described as "beautiful" or "pretty" rather than "sexy." Being sexy is a good thing, when sex is a real option in marriage, but until then, your clothing (including workout attire and swimsuits, if you're wearing them in front of men) shouldn't look similar to lingerie. By the way, *this all goes for men too*: there's a reason trashy romance novels marketed to women usually have a shirtless man on the cover! If you're in mixed company, you shouldn't look as if you're in your underwear.

Interestingly, St. Francis de Sales emphasizes cleanliness and neatness more than almost anything else in his section on modesty in dress (Part Three, Chapter 25). Circling back around to the basics: for both men and women, when you go somewhere you might meet "eligibles," at least make sure you've practiced good hygiene and done your laundry. Look and smell fresh!

Mate Material

In the fascinating (though very secular) book, *This Is Your Brain on Birth Control*, Sarah E. Hill, Ph.D., describes several studies that have shown that men are less attracted to women who are on hormonal birth control. It seems that women look, sound, move, and smell different when they are either in a non-fertile phase of their menstrual cycles, or on birth control (which essentially keeps your body in a perpetual false pregnancy). Men subconsciously pick up on this and find those women a little less attractive. They're not fertile, so they're not mate material.

Also, some studies suggest that being on birth control changes which men women find attractive and whom they choose as mates. Some women are more attracted to less stereotypically masculine-looking men when on the pill, and others are simply less interested in sex and men overall when on the pill. If you are on hormonal birth control for any reason, such as painful periods, acne, or polycystic ovarian syndrome (PCOS), it is well worth trying to get off of it, most importantly because of the many risks and side effects associated with the synthetic hormones in the pill, but also because it might be affecting your dating life. Seek out medical professionals certified in NaPro, FEMM, or another natural and fertility-friendly women's health methodology who can help treat the root of the problem and get you off birth control safely.

Put Your Eggs in Many Baskets

In his book *How to Get a Date Worth Keeping*, dating coach Dr. Henry Cloud lists lots of places he sent his clients to meet people and hit their quota of five "eligibles" per week. The grocery store, laundromat, coffee shop, gym, and dog park are all possibilities. As I mentioned before, I know of a couple who met in a grocery store parking lot because the woman noticed a cute guy and decided to make eye contact with him for a little longer than usual. He noticed and struck up a conversation, and today they're married.

There are so many places to meet a spouse, both expected and unexpected. I know several people who met their spouses through Catholic organizations and conferences (such as Life Teen camp, the National Conference for Single Catholics, Young Catholic Professionals, and Singles for Christ), and at least one couple who met through a non-Catholic event for people who vote Republican (she wasn't Catholic initially but soon converted). My parents were introduced through a mutual friend, and I initially met Enrique at a birthday party. Lots and lots of people meet at wedding receptions and parties; maybe the next time you're invited to a distant relative's celebration you don't particularly want to go to, you'll meet the love of your life! I even knew a guy who had a knack for getting dates through public transportation: he once had a whole date during an airport layover, and he met another young lady at a bus stop. If you have the right attitude and a little courage, it's possible!

Of course, there's a fine line between getting obsessed with finding someone to date everywhere you go, and simply being open to the possibility. Try to go primarily to places and events you will actually enjoy, whether you get a date or not. But try to go everywhere with willingness to walk through any door God might open. If you're a man, be willing to talk to women wherever you go and to take the risk of asking one out if she interests you, but without allowing yourself to become dismissive of women you don't find attractive. For women, same thing: be willing to talk to men wherever you go, or at least to smile and make eye contact (possibly more than you think is normal!) so that they know to come and talk to you. But try not to come home discouraged if the cute guy you saw across the room didn't come talk to you; if you enjoyed your time and "got out there," it wasn't a waste.

Don't put all your eggs in one basket by thinking that one event or method is going to get you a date or a spouse right away. Just enrich your intellectual, spiritual, social, emotional, and physical life by try-ing new things, continuing with what you enjoy, and meeting new people. Put your best foot forward, with openness to either outcome: date or no date.

Speaking of dates, what exactly is a date, and what do you do after you've gotten one? That's for the next chapter.

4

. . . .

Just Get to Know People

Be Friends, But Not "Just Friends"

Once, I had a guy friend . . . just a friend. He had mentioned going to seminary. But we wound up spending time one-on-one together pretty regularly. I started developing what one of my housemates calls a "proximity crush." Luckily, it faded as soon as we had a little distance from each other.

But, around the same time, a female friend of mine was stuck in an awkward scenario: she had fallen hard for a wonderful guy, but he saw her as only a friend . . . and continued spending time with her, never considering that she might develop a proximity crush on him. Over the next few years, two different guy friends (who had previously said we were "just friends") confessed their love to me. Soon after that, another female friend of mine thoroughly friendzoned a guy she had just met, only to fall hard for him a few months later, and then struggle with how or whether to bring it up to him.

What's the point of all these stories? To show that male-female friendships are confusing, starting with the possibility that they might not even exist. It's rare to impossible for these friendships to remain *just* friendships on both sides, no matter how much one person insists it's possible. "So-and-so is great, but I would never date him (or her)," we say, while we complain about being single.

But when we are attracted to someone from the beginning, we want to dive straight into the deep end, blitzing past any "just-friends" stuff. Once, I went out for coffee with a guy I had only met a couple of times (there was no pre-existing friendship). At the end of the date, I floated home on a cloud. He was so easy to talk to, so gentlemanly, so Catholic! I could already see myself marrying him. Within a week or two, I knew, just *knew* he was the one ... but he wasn't. We broke up within six months.

Why do we so often dive into the deep end of romance (and get our hearts broken) or stay stuck in the friendzone? Why are the people we see as friends and the people we're willing to date so mutually exclusive? I think sometimes the messages we've imbibed as Catholics are partly to blame. We're taught to "date for marriage" and "be intentional," and, in an effort to follow that advice, Catholics sometimes think they should skip over the shallower beginnings of a relationship and jump straight into preparing for matrimony.

But "intentionality" messaging works the other way too. If we don't intend to dive into the deep end and prepare to marry someone, we believe we shouldn't date him or her at all. At that point, we have two other options: we can avoid a deep connection entirely, or we can claim to be "just friends" while spending so much time together that everyone thinks we're dating.

We have so many words for these situations: terms like "talking," "situationship," "friendlationship," or "just friends." The unspoken assumption behind all these terms is that "friends" and "more than friends" are two different roads we could travel with someone of the opposite sex, and we need to stand still at the intersection until we decide which one we want to go down.

In reality, "more than friends" *includes* friendship, as the phrase implies. A romance isn't healthy if it doesn't include friendship. And, for single men and women who aren't relatives, friendship *always* includes the possibility of more than friendship. We need to recognize these realities and be open about them upfront. I've learned this the hard way, several times over, but I'm here to share the lessons with you in the form of another principle. I call it the "just get to know people" principle.

Shallow Can Be Good

When we hear the word "shallow" applied to a person, it's usually a bad thing. We certainly don't want to have a shallow relationship with a significant other, right? Actually, shallow can be good, as a preparation for deep. And "dating for marriage" or "being intentional" doesn't mean you have to decide whether someone might be spouse material within the first few times you meet. That's not a natural, healthy, or holy way to relate to other human beings.

Let me illustrate what I mean by taking some of the statements I hear Catholics make about dating and applying them to same-sex friendship scenarios:

- Lilah says, "That new girl Paola asked me to grab coffee this weekend, but I said no. I'm just not interested in being best friends with her for life."

- Jacob says, "Nate seems cool at first glance, but I don't know whether he'd be a good fit to be my roommate. What if he's a complete slob or even a thief? I don't want to waste his time or mine by asking him to hang out if he's not a good person to live with long-term."

- Katelyn says, "I had drinks with my new classmate yesterday. I know it sounds crazy, but I think she's meant to be my best friend forever!"

Doesn't this all sound a little over-the-top? Lilah doesn't know Paola very well yet, so how can she already know she's not interested in being her best friend for life? Shouldn't she just spend some time with her and then see where the friendship goes? Similarly, the best way for Jacob to find out whether Nate, who seems so cool on the surface, is a good roommate or a thief is to spend some time with him and get to know his character and habits. That's not a waste of time for either person. Katelyn is an opposite but equally strange case. What does she even mean when she says that her new classmate is "meant to be" her best friend forever? Why is that top-of-mind when she's just grabbing a drink with a new acquaintance?

Now translate all of this back into dating terms, and these

sentences will probably sound familiar:

- Lilah says, "That new guy Paul asked me out for coffee this weekend, but I said no. I'm just not interested in dating him. I could never marry him."

- Jacob says, "Kate's pretty, and I found out she's single . . . but I don't know if she's a good fit for me. What if we don't agree politically, or she's not very devout? I don't want to waste her time or mine by taking her on a date if I'm not sure I can see myself with her long-term."

- Katelyn says, "I had drinks with a new guy yesterday. I know it sounds crazy, but I think he's my future husband!"

These are examples of people diving straight into the deep end, instead of wading in step by step. Katelyn is diving into the deep end in a more obvious way, by emotionally committing to a man she barely knows. But Lilah and Jacob are also diving into the deep end by going straight to a decision they just don't have enough information for yet—to marry or not to marry, or at least, to get into a serious, long-term relationship or not. Or, more accurately, they are standing perpetually on the diving board, afraid of the chilly twelve-foot depths, when there's a perfectly good two-foot kiddy zone nearby.

Often, I believe, people allow either fear (of hurting someone, of being hurt, or of commitment in general) or pride (thinking they already know what's best for themselves and the people they date) to prematurely squash what could have been a fine, healthy relationship, whether or not it led to marriage.

This is an important point: a romance done right can be a good thing even if it doesn't end in marriage. It's okay to wade into the shallows even if you're not sure you want to go all the way to the deep end. It's okay to get to know someone not knowing whether you want to end up married to him or her. How else will you find out? That's discernment. That's real intentionality. As a Reddit user named Daniel put it, "It is okay even to *love* someone you don't end up being with." Just get to know someone, and see where God leads you.

Secret Admirers, in Plain Sight

If going on even one date means we'll have to either marry the person or break his or her heart (and incur an accusation of "leading someone on"), we feel it's best to know the person very well and see that there's definite marriage potential before going on a date. So we stay in the friendzone for a while.

This is actually recommended sometimes in Christian/Catholic circles. Maybe it stems from the *I Kissed Dating Goodbye* trend of the nineties or maybe it's advice intended for teenagers that somehow got carried over into early adulthood. Sometimes there's a vague sense that being friends is wholesome and safe, while dating is a little icky and secular. So we make friends with a love interest and hang out for a while, hoping he or she also sees what a wonderful couple we'll make when the time is right. Or we have no romantic interest, but we enjoy having a friend of the opposite sex, and we're sure he or she feels exactly as we do.

It's a controversial thing to say, but I'll say it: men and women can't be friends, in the sense of deep one-on-one friendship, without at least one of them falling in love with the other. Picture friendship and romance not as two options, a fork in the road, but as two stages of the same journey. If a man and a woman are walking together, spending time one-on-one, deepening their relationship, their friendship *will* ultimately develop into romance on at least one side—or at least some twisted form of friendship that excludes other romantic connections.

Think about it: why is it inappropriate for a person who's married or in a serious relationship to spend significant time one-on-one with someone else of the opposite sex? Because time spent one-on-one together (or talking on the phone or texting) is time walking down the road, deepening the emotional connection. If marriage is not a possibility for two people, they need to stop walking together, because the alternative is temptation and heartbreak for at least one person.

I used to think there were lots of exceptions to the rule that one person will always fall in love, but I have been proven wrong over and over, through others' experience and my own experience. I can't put it better than comedian Elyse Myers who says (in a video called "First

Heartbreak"): "If you present your friendship as the exception, all it will tell me is that it's your *friend* who's the one in love."

I've seen or participated in these male-female "friendlationships" many times. One person was always being tortured by hidden feelings and the desire to walk further down the road toward marriage. Maybe he or she was even attempting to lead the other person along the road bit by bit, but with subtlety instead of straightforwardness. Inevitably, when the truth finally came out, it resulted in the loss of *both* the hope of a future marriage and the friendship.

Sometimes women are shocked or even angry when their male friends confess romantic feelings. But this is actually perfectly normal and natural. Every instinct in a man is designed to prompt him to pursue women and produce offspring, and "just friends" doesn't cut it. Sometimes men will go along with the idea of dating the female friend who confesses her feelings—but not for long. As matchmaker Alessandra Conti said on the podcast *Dating in the City*, a hunter is more invested in the deer he went out and hunted than the deer who voluntarily lies down on his doorstep.

There is only one road, with stages that must be walked in order, and it's just a matter of how far down you wish to walk with someone. Dating done right is just friendship, *plus* the explicit possibility of marriage.

The Stages of a Relationship

So what are the stages of a relationship? There's no single, definitive number of stages, but it's pretty clear that getting engaged and getting married are big steps that bring you into a new stage. The earlier part of getting to know someone is more of a continuous spectrum, but it's helpful to define some zones within that spectrum using specific terminology. Here are perspectives from a few experts:

From a psychologist

Dr. Mario Sacasa, a Catholic psychologist, lists five stages in his online course *Dating Well*: friendship, dating, boyfriend/girlfriend, engaged, and married. He defines friendship as the stage where you enjoy each other's company and have good conversations, but no romantic feelings. Dating is the stage of initial romantic interest, "just beginning to put the feelers out, maybe going on a couple dates with people, maybe going on dates with a couple people at once," says Sacasa. Boyfriend/girlfriend is, of course, the more serious and exclusive stage of dating when you're explicitly discerning marriage, and engaged and married are fairly self-explanatory. He emphasizes that each stage builds on the previous one: "When you're dating, you should still be friends. A healthy marriage continues that sense of discovery found in dating."

From a priest

Fr. Chad Ripperger, a priest popular online for his very traditional stance and YouTube sermons on various topics, lists four stages in his talk "Four Stages of Courtship": friendship, courtship, engagement, and marriage. He defines the friendship stage as a non-exclusive stage with no physical affection or time alone; courtship as a stage where exclusivity begins and the two people are more openly discerning whether the other person has the virtues to be a good spouse and parent, and helping each other grow in virtue; the engagement stage as, of course, the stage when the two people have made a decision and are preparing for marriage (including by increasing their emotional bond and physical affection); and marriage as a permanent sacramental commitment.

From a matchmaker

Cristina Pineda, her sister and cofounder Alessandra Conti, and their team of matchmakers at Matchmakers in the City usually speak of four stages: dating, relationship or boyfriend/girlfriend, engaged, and married. Dating is the stage when you're going on dates but aren't expecting exclusivity, so you might be going on dates with more than one person. Relationship or boyfriend/girlfriend is a more serious, exclusive stage of dating. Engaged and married are what you'd expect. When I interviewed Pineda, she emphasized to me that dating or courtship doesn't begin until the first date: "'We're talking' doesn't count. Until you go on a date, it's nothing."

What they have in common

Despite coming from different backgrounds and areas of expertise, all these experts have some things in common. They all recommend starting off with friendship and/or non-exclusive dating (the shallows), before moving into discerning marriage with one person. At first glance, it looks as if the priest and the psychologist recommend building a "just friends" friendship first, while the matchmakers encourage jumping straight into dating, but I think this is a surface-level difference. Because friendship and romance are both part of the road to a happy marriage, you always have to build a friendship, whether you do it by going on dates or not. (For grown men and women, especially those who are not naturally thrown together by school or work, I side with the matchmakers and recommend going on dates from the beginning. I'll explain why later in the chapter.)

Lots of people try to do the stages out of order, getting too exclusive or too close to marriage too soon. There are a few different ways to do this. One is by letting the emotions and/or physical affection jump ahead to a later stage of the relationship, and another is by letting the intellect jump ahead to a later stage.

Out of Order Emotionally and/or Physically

This can look like spending too much time together, revealing too much "deep stuff" about oneself too soon and creating emotional intimacy too quickly, or too much physical affection that doesn't correspond to your commitment level. These can all feed off each other: if you're physically affectionate with someone (even at the level of hugs and hand-holding), you usually feel more emotionally attached. And spending lots of time alone together often leads to intimate late-night conversations and more physical affection. These things aren't necessarily bad or sinful (unless you're violating chastity), but they might be happening out of order, before you've seen someone's character and built adequate trust.

How do you make sure you're going in order? Set some healthy boundaries for yourself. You don't need an excessive number of inflexible rules to cover every scenario, but you should have a few pretty firm guidelines for yourself and be confident enough to express them to the person you're dating, when necessary. To help you decide what those boundaries should be, here's some expert advice.

Conversation boundaries

To pace your emotional intimacy and self-revelation, Pineda recommends writing out three lists of conversation topics: one list that you'd be willing to talk about on a first date, one that you will save until you're in an exclusive relationship with someone, and one that you will save until you're engaged or close to getting engaged. (The exact topics of conversation in each list won't be the same for everyone, but I think it's helpful to consider what *you* are normally comfortable sharing with a new acquaintance versus a close friend.)

When she spoke at our Nashville singles' event, Pineda discouraged talking about religion or politics on a first date, beyond simply sharing that you're Catholic and faith is important to you—nothing too personal or controversial. If you're seeing the person you're on a date with as primarily a person you're getting to know, not too different from a friend, it should be natural to spend your first few dates asking primarily about interests, hobbies, work, and travel. You're trying to find things you have in common rather than treating your date as a therapist or a debate opponent.

Time boundaries

Pacing the amount of time you spend with your new love interest is important too, and makes it easier to pace everything else. It's pretty unhealthy to meet new friends and start spending every waking moment with them instantly, so don't do that with dating, either. Pineda recommends going on dates about once a week in the non-exclusive dating phase.

Also, I recommend keeping up the activities and other friendships you developed when you formed your well-rounded life and practiced the "just meet people" principle. If you have a reasonably busy social calendar and you're prioritizing your prayer life and other duties like work or school, you have only so much time left, so going on dates about once a week or less will probably feel easy. Not to mention, you might also have dates with other people (more on dating multiple people in the next chapter). As you move toward exclusivity, you will naturally spend more and more time together, especially as you integrate into each other's friend groups and meet each other's families. As one of my housemates put it recently, try not to "overdose on each other" at the beginning, or you might find yourselves burning out quickly. Slow and steady usually wins the race.

Physical boundaries

Physical touch is a big, difficult subject, and I have a whole chapter on it later. For now, of course, keep in mind you should not dive into the deep end by having sex in any stage of the relationship before marriage. But you also shouldn't dive straight into the middle part of the pool. Even if it's not a matter of official Church teaching, it's imprudent to rush other gestures like kissing.

A friend shared with me that a guy she liked used to touch her all the time—holding her hand, touching her hair, etc.—which kept her very interested in him. It feels wonderful to be loved and desired through touch! But sadly, he never actually dated her or had any real intention of discerning marriage, so the emotional attachment was fruitless. Physical affection should *express* trust and emotional intimacy that already exists, rather than *create* an emotional attachment.

Out of Order Intellectually: No "Spouse Interviews"

As I mentioned earlier, we Catholics often hear that we're supposed to "date intentionally" and "date for marriage," and "know what we're looking for." This is good advice when it's rightly understood, but we often take it too far. We decide what we're looking for in a spouse and then spend our first dates (or the pre-date "talking phase") trying to find out as quickly as possible whether the other person meets our standards and is wife or husband "material." And the qualities we are looking for are sometimes unrealistic and unnecessary, or not what actually will make us happy and holy.

I understand firsthand why we tend to do this. We have an enormous fear of anything that smells like "leading someone on," and we also fear heartbreak, understandably. And we sometimes have long wishlists of traits because we believe this will ensure a happy marriage. If there is a dealbreaker, we want to find it, break contact, and move on to someone else before too much time is wasted. Ultimately, it's an effort to control the outcome of our lives, rather than putting God in control.

Plus, this approach—quickly testing your date for compatibility against your own "dealbreaker list"—isn't exactly romantic. Daniel from Reddit told me that the early stage of dating seemed like a "job interview" rather than a relationship. In his honor, I'm nicknaming this the "spouse interview approach." And it's the wrong approach, for a couple of reasons.

Reason #1: virtue is a hidden gem

First, it's simply impossible to find out the most important things about a person within the first few dates. As Fr. Ripperger emphasizes, and as common sense shows, the best spouses are people of good character, people with virtue. The only way to really know a person's character is to observe what they do. What people say about themselves is not reliable enough. Even if someone isn't a liar, we fallen human beings aren't the best judges of ourselves, and we very often speak of ourselves in aspirational ways.

For instance, if a man were to ask me on a first date, "So, what do you like to do with your free time?" I would mention reading, writing, baking bread, and taking rosary walks around the neighborhood, all of which are true—I do *like* those things. But if he were to spend time with me over the course of a few months, he would see that I struggle to find time to bake bread or read because I spend so much time searching online for the perfect pair of shoes. Similarly, I remember a man I dated saying (I'm sure, with perfect sincerity) that whenever he did something important, he always thought it through and had a definite reason for doing it. Yet, as I got to know him over the months of our relationship and heard more about the decisions he had actually made, I discovered he was a lot more spontaneous and less definite in his goals than he thought he was. That wasn't necessarily a moral flaw in him, but it illustrates that even good people are not perfect at self-portrayal. There's no substitute for time—slowly, steadily getting to know someone.

Reason #2: it's objectifying

Second, the spouse interview approach is rather objectifying. When we hear "objectifying," we usually think of the way the secular culture around us treats people, especially women, but there are other ways to treat a person as an object.

The secular world thinks it's okay to make dates a functional affair, a formality in order to get to sexual pleasure as soon as possible. I believe many Catholics have also fallen into the mindset that it's okay to make dates a functional affair, a formality in order to find a spouse without wasting time or risking heartache. The secular attitude thinks it's okay to compare someone's body to unrealistic standards—maybe airbrushed models, maybe a daydream—and then dismiss someone for not being attractive enough. The Catholic with a "spouse interview" approach thinks it's okay to compare someone's personality, background, opinions, skills, etc. to a standard that might be unrealistic—maybe a "tradwife" account on Instagram, maybe a daydream, maybe a fictional book or movie—and then dismiss someone for not measuring up. (And sometimes, we throw in some physical comparisons too.) There's that "shopping mindset" again that I mentioned in Chapter Two: making a list and analyzing people like items on a shelf.

Have you ever purchased something that was exactly what you wanted, and then been dissatisfied with it? I've been in a relationship with someone who checked every box on my list, yet the relationship became miserable. There were things standing in our way that I'd never thought to put on my list. I mentioned that we fallen humans are not always good at describing ourselves accurately, and by the same token, we are not always good at knowing what or *who* will make us happy and holy. The whole point of marriage, or of any relationship, is that it draws you out of yourself and changes you for the better.

This is the final reason why starting with that "shopping list" can actually set you up for failure. You might have entirely the wrong traits on your list. Or you might have a number of objectively good traits—I did, in the past relationship I just mentioned—but be blinded to deeper problems in the relationship, because you keep pointing to your list and saying, "But he (or she) checks every box, so he (or she) has to be the perfect person for me!"

Remember, your date isn't applying for the job of being your spouse, and you're not the boss. Don't interview your dates. Instead, just get to know people. The same interviewee who mentioned the "shopping mindset" summed it up well when he said, "A relationship is just two people relating." Be a person getting to know another person. Relate to him or her as you would to any other new acquaintance, and use your list of first-date appropriate topics as a guideline to keep yourself on track if you're tempted to overshare in a way that you know you'll regret later. After each date, you can reflect, with the Lord's help, on whether spending more time with that person seems prudent and pleasant. If not, no harm done, because you kept your boundaries. Just as it never hurts to meet people, it rarely hurts to get to know someone at least a little bit. An image of God is not a waste of time.

Friendly Hangouts vs. Dates

As promised, here's my take on whether men and women should be just friends first, and then proceed to dating, or just go on dates from the start.

This is an area where there's no wrong way, really. People find themselves in many different situations, and happy marriages can come out of either scenario. However, if you are an adult and already have an inkling of romantic interest in someone, I highly recommend going on dates from the beginning.

First, unless you happen to work closely together or have a similar class schedule on a small campus, it's just hard to get to know someone very well as a young adult without intentionally planning a day, time, and place to get together and chat. And that's exactly what a date is.

Second, I think calling those planned chats "dates" avoids a lot of confusion and pain. If you have any romantic feelings, you're not just friends, so why pretend to be? Why allow the other person to think you're just friends if you're not? Why torture yourself with wondering whether he or she has any romantic interest or not? I know that we women are prone to going to our friends and talking over every small interaction with a crush, always asking, "Do you think he likes me? Am I reading too much into this?" I don't know whether men do the same thing, but I'm sure they at least spend time wondering about the signs they're getting from their crush. It might be thrilling for a little while to dwell in the suspense, but eventually, it can become anxiety-inducing and a huge waste of time.

Next, as I mentioned before, it is very common for women to think they can be just friends with men, only to find out later that the men like them romantically, and vice-versa. The chances that both the man and the woman are secretly in love with each other and ready to express that at the same time are slim, which means the chances of disappointment, confusion, awkwardness, and pain are very high. So I recommend starting off with going on dates, which makes it clear that there's a hint of romantic interest; but be sure to make it clear that a date doesn't mean diving into the deep end.

For men, this means asking out every woman you're even a little interested in, rather than allowing a "just friends" relationship to form. You can use some language to make it clear that your goal with the date is just to get to know her a little and not to dive straight into an exclusive relationship. (Look back at the "default to yes" portion of Chapter One for a script.)

For women, this means declining to hang out one-on-one with a guy unless it's a date. If he asks to hang out, you can ask, "Is this a group thing, or just us?" if that's not already clear. If it will just be the two of you, you can say, "I have a rule for myself that I don't hang out one-on-one with guys unless it's a date, to avoid any confusion or gossip." If you're open to a date with him, you might want to add some extra encouragement by saying, "But I see a date as just a chance to get to know someone and see if something more develops, so I'm open to a date if you are!"

Of course, these dates should initially be focused on building friendship, but building it as a foundation for a possible romance and eventual marriage. I'll talk more about this early stage of dating—the non-exclusive stage—in the next chapter.

5

. . . .

The Non-Exclusive Stage

Who Says You Shouldn't "Date Around"?

When I ran my first speed dating event, someone who had signed up contacted me to cancel her registration, saying that she was "talking to" someone now. I wasn't in a position to give her life advice, but I wanted to ask, "Why can't you talk to more than one guy?"

Relationships happen in stages. The first stage of a man-woman relationship that might lead to marriage is building a friendship, often through a non-exclusive dating stage. Exclusivity shouldn't be expected and taken for granted. And it doesn't need to be given to someone who hasn't asked for it (much less someone who is merely "talking to" you). Yes, this is permission, and even encouragement, to date multiple people at once.

Does that sound strange, or icky, or maybe even immoral? Let's do another translation test, putting it in friendship terms. Say you and Josh (or Jessica), whom you recently met at a party, decide to go for a hike on Saturday morning. Then, after Mass on Sunday, you meet Blaise (or Bella), who also seems interested in hanging out and becoming friends. In a friendship context, would you ever say to yourself, "I can't hang out with Blaise because I just hung out with Josh, and

I don't know yet whether Josh will be my best friend for life"? I hope not, because that would be intense and strange. Yet Catholics do this in dating all the time.

I assume it's because of the same "intentionality" and "date for marriage" messages we've heard, but again, the messages have been twisted. Scripture and Church teaching show us that we may only *marry* one person, until death. This means we should never be engaged to more than one person at a time, and it implies that at some point, probably before engagement, we've built a deeper relationship with one person. But God never revealed any particular rules for dating, and certainly never said that we couldn't go on dates with more than one person for a while before focusing on the one.

So, in the first stage of dating, you should probably be willing to date multiple people at once, usually for two to three months. When I first started dating, I felt icky about this myself, but I've been completely converted, and I think my conversion to non-exclusive dating was a big part of how I ended up engaged to a wonderful man today. Read on to understand how I was converted and why this non-exclusive stage of up to 90 days is so important.

Ask the Experts

Remember the experts from the last chapter (matchmakers, a priest, and a psychologist) who advocated for a non-exclusive phase of dating? In the last few years of my dating journey, I kept running into more people who advocated for this, or simply assumed that such a phase was normal.

Dr. Henry Cloud, the Christian psychologist who wrote *How to Get a Date Worth Keeping*, advocates for going on dates with several people before "getting serious." Husband-and-wife team Kait Warman and JJ Tomlin, hosts of the *Heart of Dating* podcast, encourage something similar, particularly for people who struggle with over-committing too soon. A philosophy professor at my college discouraged us from pairing off too soon after arriving on campus freshman year. Interestingly, when I've talked with my own parents and grandparents about dating, they seemed to assume that "dating around" was normal until things "got serious" or you decided to "go steady." When I mentioned the topic of the non-exclusive phase to my editor for this book, he mentioned that it sounded like "very good advice." Amazingly, the experts I've found almost universally agree on two to three months being a good amount of time to date someone before moving to the exclusive phase.

Matchmaker Cristina Pineda explained to me what this three-month phase looks like. "You're seeing each other maybe once a week," she said, "and the man's almost always asking out. The woman can invite after maybe a few dates. . . . But the man should be driving that courtship phase."

Pineda also says that, as long as the couple haven't slept together, the man will naturally bring up the topic of exclusivity, usually before the three-month mark, "because the man will want to lock you down for himself." Although a man might want to ask sooner, and many women might be open to exclusivity sooner, Pineda strongly recommends getting to know someone for at least two months, preferably three, before making that commitment and closing oneself off to other people. If he asks sooner, the woman could simply say, "I am so enjoying getting to know you, but for myself, I have a three-month rule before I get into an exclusive relationship," said Pineda.

From personal experience, I said something similar to my now-fiancé when we first went out, before he ever asked me to be his girlfriend. I phrased it more like, "I am getting to know a few different people right now and trying to give myself about three months to discern whether to get into a serious relationship with anyone." He respected that decision, and it gave him a hint about when he could ask me to be his girlfriend and expect a yes, if we were still seeing each other by then.

What should dates look like during this phase? Dr. Kerry Cronin of Boston College is famous for her talks on dating and gives her students this assignment: go on a real date (as opposed to a hookup or an ambiguous hangout). In the documentary *The Dating Project*, Cronin outlines several levels of dates and shares how a couple might move from one level to the next over time. A "level one" date is similar to a one-on-one hangout as friends, although Cronin emphasizes that the person who invites pays. (She also says that the date should cost no more than ten dollars. While inflation or the city you live in might have to push this to twenty or thirty, this is an important tip for the guys especially: start smaller, simpler, and less expensive, keeping the date low-pressure.)

Cronin also emphasizes that there should be no physical affection beyond an "A-frame hug": that is, shoulders are coming closer together, but everything below that stays apart. Most importantly for this chapter, Cronin says that you can be going on level one dates with several people at once. "No saliva has been exchanged!" she quips to her students in the documentary.

If the idea of dating several people still feels icky to you by this point in the chapter, I challenge you to ask yourself why. What could possibly be gross or immoral about having a milkshake with Mandy on Thursday and then seeing a movie with Molly on Friday? If you're not kissing or talking about what to name your future children, you're essentially friends, and it's okay to have more than one friend, even if you are intentionally allowing for the possibility that romance could blossom with one of your friends.

Also, think back to the funnel example from Chapter One. Meeting lots of new eligibles is filling the top of your funnel. Going on first dates with the ones who pique your interest or ask you out is the next part of the funnel, which will probably already be a lot narrower than the top. If you meet twenty new people, five of them might spark your interest at least a little. At this point, you don't have enough information to choose which of those five will be the best fit for you, so you would be wise to get to know each of them, usually by going on a few more dates. The funnel doesn't have to be narrowed from twenty down to one all at once. It can be narrowed more gradually, allowing you some time to discern.

"Dating around" tends to have a negative connotation and be set up in opposition to "dating for marriage" or "dating intentionally." But I believe this step-by-step process, a gradual narrowing of the funnel, is part of *truly* intentional dating. Done right, it gives people a better shot at finding a good spouse without unnecessary heartbreak than the now-normal approach where exclusivity is expected right away.

A counselor I used to see once told me, "People today don't really date. They have mini-marriages." That means every breakup is a mini-divorce. (Depending on how young you start the pattern of mini-marriage and mini-divorce, you might have a lot of practice with it by the time your real marriage happens. Is it any wonder real divorce is so common?) Dating a few people at a time can help keep you out of the mini-marriage mindset and help you be intentional about which of your dating connections you want to nurture into a real marriage.

The Day-to-Day of Dating Several People

Think back to Chapter One, "You Don't Have a Type." Is that statement starting to make more sense now? You can safely get to know many types, or enjoy spending time with many people, without taking advantage of them physically or emotionally, if you follow the pointers that Pineda and Cronin suggest:

- **Don't make the date too long**. Cronin challenges her students to keep it below 90 minutes, and Pineda recommends no more than two hours for a first date.

- **Don't make the date too expensive.** This will vary by your location, age, and other factors, so the exact cost is not too important. What is important is that you make the date a pleasant, conversational experience without making it high-pressure or blowing your budget. Instead of dinner on a first date, Pineda recommends small plates and drinks (not too many drinks, and they don't have to be alcoholic), or getting ice cream and taking a walk in a nice part of town. Many people choose coffee for a first date, but Pineda cautions against making it too much like a job interview. (If coffee is what you can afford, try to jazz it up: get it to-go and walk to a bench by the river, so you're looking at a nice view side-by-side.)

- **Don't make the date too emotionally intimate, but have something to talk about.** Remember the three lists Pineda recommends? Both Pineda and Cronin also recommend coming up with a few appropriate conversation-starting questions before your date so that you won't freeze up. At our singles' event, Pineda especially recommended that men have questions ready, and that women let the man lead the conversation a bit more, keeping him in the pursuer role. Here's a quick personal story: I once made the mistake of charging into a first date armed with lots of questions because I already perceived the man as shy and wanted to avoid awkward silences. Unfortunately, after the date, I felt uninterested because of how shy he seemed, while he thought the date had gone great because of how easily conversation flowed! If I had let him lead a little more, we both would probably have had a more accurate idea of each other. Besides, there's nothing bad about a little silence now and then.

- **Don't make the date too physically intimate.** Again, there should be no physical touch beyond a simple, non-intimate, friendship-type hug. (Even that isn't necessary at this stage if you're not comfortable with it. Different people have different feelings about touch.) If it's hard to tell whether a certain gesture (e.g., touching your date's arm or holding hands) is too much for a level-one, non-exclusive date, just think about whether you'd want to do the same to someone else tomorrow, or whether what you're doing will make it awkward to see the person again if you decide not to continue dating. (Again, a whole chapter on physical affection is coming later.)

Honesty with Tact

Do you have to tell your dates that you're dating other people? The experts differ a bit on this.

According to Pineda, there's no need. She doesn't recommend dating several people from the same social circle who might run into each other and accidentally find out, making things awkward. Even though there's nothing wrong with going out with more than one person at a time, you don't want those people to feel as if they're in direct competition with each other. Pineda often says that, while on a date, you should "make your date feel like the only person in the world" (pointing out that many saints, such as Mother Teresa, were known for making each person they spoke to feel that special). You don't *have* to tell.

Interestingly, my grandparents, Dr. Cloud, and other people who dated several decades ago didn't have to think about this question, because, in their day, exclusivity was not *assumed*. It had to be asked for and granted. Everyone knew that all their classmates were going on dates with each other, and it wasn't a big deal—it's just what everyone did on the weekends. But clearly, this is not quite the situation we're in today.

On the other hand, Kait Warman and JJ Tomlin of *Heart of Dating* recommend being transparent and telling all the people you're dating that you are also seeing other people. In a podcast episode called "Dating Multiple People as a Christian," Tomlin acknowledges that it's always possible for the other person to feel unsure about you going on dates with others. "You have to be clear and firm in your 'why,'" says Tomlin. "Your character will shine over time. . . . And then, ultimately, it's out of your control how they respond or maybe judge you."

Warman adds, "The right person will be ignited to want to try to pursue you and want to be with you. The right person is not going to be so turned off by this." She also shares in the same episode that she met JJ during a ninety-day dating challenge she gave herself, inspired by Dr. Cloud. She went on dates with a total of four men over the course of 90 days, and confesses that she probably wouldn't have gone on a date with JJ at all if she hadn't been challenging herself to be more open. It turned out to be the best first date of her life. Right after their first date, however, she shared that she was also going on dates with other men because she had a history of over-committing too quickly and ending up in unhealthy relationships. JJ respected that. It's a good idea to examine yourself and understand why spending a few months in the non-exclusive stage is a good idea for you, so that you can share that "why" with your dates if and when you choose.

Personally, I recommend being transparent with your dates. When I attempted to go on dates with more than one man without telling any of them that this was happening, I found it very stressful. Although I knew I wasn't doing anything wrong, I also knew that what I was doing could be easily misunderstood by guys who didn't have the same perspective on the non-exclusive stage of dating. As Warman and Tomlin say in the aforementioned episode, everyone decides for themselves, based on whatever they happen to have heard or experienced, what the "rules" for Christian dating are, so everyone's approach is different. I felt I needed to explain what I was doing to preserve my own honesty and treat my dates fairly.

I also knew that the Catholic community in my area was very close-knit; I would hardly be able to find any Catholics in a hundred-mile radius who wouldn't know each other and mention their dates with me on the gossip grapevine. I fully understood why most people in my Catholic community would almost rather not go on dates at all than risk being considered a "player" or a "flirt" by going out with more than one person. After all, that could ruin *all* the potential relationships you've started. If you've tried dating on a Catholic campus or in any other close-knit community, you probably feel the same fear.

So, especially after hearing this *Heart of Dating* episode (which came out around the same time that I was embarking on my own ninety-day challenge of sorts), I decided to tell each man I went out with that I didn't want to go straight into an exclusive relationship. No matter how awkward it felt to tell a man something like, "I'm interested in you, but I'm also interested in other people," it would be less awkward than a man telling me, "I heard you're also dating so-and-so; what's going on with that?"

When I ran and attended my first speed dating event and decided to "default to yes" with the men there, I also challenged myself to *remain* open to every guy until I saw a particular reason to close the door, or until he closed the door for me. The *maximum* amount of time I would continue to date the same person non-exclusively would be three months, but for me (similar to Warman's history), the challenge was to avoid getting carried away into over-commitment too soon. Telling myself I had to be open to everyone for about three months was a healthy challenge.

As with many things, though, men and women may need to handle this situation differently.

For women

My approach as a woman was something like this. If I had a good date or two with a guy, and he asked me out again, I'd respond with something like, "I'm open to another date, but I just want to let you know that I'm getting to know a few different people right now, and I'm not ready to rush into an exclusive relationship. If you're okay with that, I'd love to go out with you again." Despite my fears, every man I was interested in going out with again acted unfazed by this script.

Feel free to borrow it, or, if you adapt it, keep a good balance of three points. First, show genuine interest in the man ("I'd love to go out with you again"). Second, say the words "not exclusive" and/or "other people" to make it clear that you're dating others, but without naming names or numbers. It would not come across well to say, "I'm also going out with your friend Timothy and two other guys I met online."

And third, respect his freedom: if he's uncomfortable with dating non-exclusively, he is under no obligation to continue dating you. If he's open to hearing it, you can *explain* further why you're doing this, but you do not need to *defend* your decision, nor does he. According to all the experts, in the non-exclusive stage, you're taking one date at a time; there's no commitment at all, and you can stop going on dates with someone for any reason at all, including the other person's approach to dating. (If you can't agree on what level of commitment you have and how a relationship should progress, you'll probably have a hard time agreeing on other things down the road.)

If a man likes you, has a healthy level of confidence in himself, and is not too controlling, he will probably respect this and continue to pursue you. Remember to hand over your dating life to the Lord regularly, asking Him to inspire your words and actions and those of the men you date, so that the best man for you will have the courage to continue pursuing and show you his character. It will probably be pretty easy to narrow your dates down to him when it's time to be exclusive.

Personally, once I was about halfway through the three months I'd envisioned, I found that my now-fiancé Enrique had pretty organically become the only one left. With each of the other gentlemen, I had either found something that didn't align and declined to go out again, or the gentleman had informed me he didn't plan to ask me out again. Meanwhile, I had found that I liked Enrique a lot—way more than I expected to when we first matched at speed dating, or even on our first date. It took our fourth and fifth dates to really solidify that I knew and liked him well enough to move into an exclusive relationship; at about that point, I casually mentioned that I wasn't currently going out with anyone else. When he asked me to be his girlfriend a few weeks later (about two and a half months after our first date), I was ready and very certain in my decision.

From there, it didn't take much longer before we were talking about engagement. The fact that I was also seeing other guys during our first few weeks of dating probably slowed down the pace of getting into an exclusive relationship, but I think, ironically, it also sped up my journey to marriage. Allowing myself that lengthier time to discern going exclusive with someone had prompted me to give Enrique more of a chance than I otherwise would have. If I felt obligated to get my funnel from twenty down to one all at once, I might have picked the wrong one. Because I narrowed it gradually, I chose someone who already had a history of being good for me. And, instead of choosing someone out of a sense of scarcity or desperation, because he was the only one around, I chose Enrique from a place of freedom, confidence, and the self-knowledge gained from reflecting on my interactions with lots of different people.

For men

Many Catholic men I know, including Enrique and my brothers, prefer dating only one woman at a time and focusing all their energy on pursuing the girl they like best at the moment. If you really only like *her*—genuinely like her, not just out of a sense of scarcity or desperation because she's the only woman you've spoken to lately—that's fine.

When I asked Pineda about navigating the non-exclusive dating stage, she told me there's no need to go out of your way to make sure you have multiple people to date (e.g., by downloading a new dating app you weren't using before or asking out women you're not really interested in). The point of the non-exclusive stage is less about how many people you're actively going out with, and more about the level of commitment you have with your date(s). Remember, during this stage, you are building friendship with the possibility of romance, taking it one date at a time. If you haven't had the exclusivity conversation with a woman yet, there's nothing wrong with asking out another woman if your interest is piqued.

Let's say you do end up going on dates with two women—or, even if you are interested in only one, you want to avoid getting serious immediately and allow the option of pursuing another. As a man, if you share this information with your dates, you'll have to be very careful about how you say it. (Unfortunately, or fortunately, men and women are very different, as you may have noticed.) You want to make the woman you're pursuing feel special and wanted, so that you're not smothering any first sparks of romance. Telling her too bluntly that you're seeing several other girls might do just that. For best results, I recommend keeping your words focused on her, rather than yourself.

Here's one option: "I really enjoyed our date last week, and I'd love to take you on another one if you're open to it. And just so you know, I am not demanding that you'll be exclusive with me right away! I just want to continue getting to know you and seeing whether we might be a good fit for a relationship."

Another option: "I'd love to take you out again. By the way, I don't want to pressure you to move too fast or make you feel like you have to be committed to me. I think it's healthy for both of us to get to know each other for a couple months before getting into an exclusive relationship. But I've really enjoyed our dates so far, and I think there's real potential here!"

The key points to include from both of these options are as follows. First, express real interest and excitement to continue spending time with her. Second, make sure she knows that you're not assuming or demanding exclusivity. I really recommend using the word "exclusive" explicitly somewhere, implying the possibility of going out with someone else.

The key things to *avoid* are, first, anything that comes across as bragging about whom or how many others you're dating, and second, anything that makes her feel as if you're comparing her to other women to see whether she's the best. (In some sense, you are, of course, but there's no need to make that the focus of the conversation.)

It may feel very strange to bring this up, and some women may sniff out the fact that you're seeing other women and dislike that. But in my experience, many women in the Catholic world fear going on a third or even a first date because they feel as if they're supposed to commit to a man right away, before they're even sure whether or not they like him. Remember that it often takes women three dates to start *feeling* any romantic or physical attraction to a man, even if they're intellectually interested in him and seeing potential. If they think that you are expecting them to be all-in from the start, and they don't *feel* all-in, they might just default to no. Women might actually be quite relieved to hear that you're not *expecting* exclusivity from them. Phrasing it in this way, to show that you are respecting *her* freedom and allowing *her* all the time she needs to make up her mind, shows thoughtfulness and can help make a woman feel more at ease. (At least, this is what I would have liked to hear from a man I was dating!)

Ending It in the Non-Exclusive Stage

Speaking of saying no, let's talk about ending your dating connections in the non-exclusive stage. I'm calling them "dating connections" because, in this stage, you are not committed to anyone, and you don't have a boyfriend or girlfriend, so in some sense, there's no such thing as a breakup. But, in my experience, it's usually better to be clear with someone that you don't plan to go out with him or her again.

For men, this usually means simply telling her politely that you don't see this turning into a serious relationship, so you don't plan to ask her out again. Wish her well, and if you see her around, try to act as polite and generically friendly as you would toward any other woman you're not interested in dating. Usually, these situations are only as awkward as we make them, and if you've kept the dates at Dr. Cronin's Level One, there's no reason for it to be awkward at all.

For women, this usually means waiting to see if the man asks you out again, and if so, politely declining and telling him that you are not interested in moving toward a serious relationship. In some situations, it might be appropriate to tell him this proactively, rather than waiting for him to ask again; for example, I usually proactively told a man I didn't want to move forward if we had gone out at least three times already and I still got the "vibe" that he was interested. I felt that he might be expecting another "yes" at that point and wanted to spare him the awkwardness of an abrupt "no" just when he thought things were going well. Use your intuition and pray to the Holy Spirit for guidance on what would be least humiliating and most charitable in each situation.

For both men and women, I recommend a phone call (or in-person conversation, if you run into them frequently anyway) rather than a text to end things, especially if you've been on more than one date. Usually, texting the person to ask for a good time to have a phone call (or asking, "Could we talk for a minute?" if you're in person) is a good idea, in my opinion, because it hints that there's something important to talk about and ensures that there's enough time to ask questions and end on good terms. I have been on the receiving end of both a "Can we talk?" text and the unexpected ending-the-connection phone call. The first scenario was much better for my state of mind; afterwards I could let go and move on more easily.

With God and Your Gut

Another important point, which Kait Warman emphasizes: prayer and reflection is very important during this stage, as it always is. While the whole point of this stage is to discern slowly, you do ultimately need to decide. It's not fair to string someone along for a full three months and then suddenly say that you're just not that interested.

So, after each date, do a check-in with God and your gut. In a journal or in your mind, chat with Jesus about your recent dates, telling Him all about them like you would a very close friend. Ask Him what He thinks: did He see red flags? Did that person bring out better sides of you or worse sides? How did you feel during and after the date? While it's not wise to make decisions based on fleeting emotions, fireworks, or doldrums, it's also not wise to ignore your emotions or even sensations in your body.

I think this is particularly important for women; the stereotype that women are more emotional and intuitive isn't entirely false! If being around a certain guy consistently gives you a sick feeling in your stomach (that isn't just nervousness about being on a date, or what your hormones happen to be doing that day), pay attention to that. If you have a joyful, peaceful desire to continue spending time with someone, continue! Keep in mind that, especially for women, that general desire to spend time with someone might grow into full-blown romantic and sexual attraction over time, even if the spark isn't fully there now.

Remember, too, that if you do become interested in more than one person, you can have overlapping three-month non-exclusive dating periods. I conveniently started off my three-month challenge with a speed dating event where I got several matches, at a time when I didn't have any existing dating connections. But you might organically meet someone in June and go on a couple of dates, then meet someone else in July and go on another date or two with each person; then by August find that the first person isn't a good fit and stop dating him or her, but continue with the second, and a third you just met . . . you get the idea. But generally, within two or three months of just getting to know someone, one date at a time, you will see if he or she is a good enough fit that it makes sense to discern marriage exclusively with him or her.

6

. . . .

Long-Distance and No-Distance Dating

How to Survive Being Separated and Avoid Being Smothered

B efore addressing the exclusive stage of dating, I want to delve into some special cases. So far, I've assumed you're dating in a generic city with in-person opportunities to meet and date people who hopefully don't know each other, but not everyone is in that position. You might meet someone who lives far away, or you might meet someone who lives a little too close to home.

In a world where many people meet online, long-distance relationships are common. However, they're still a little controversial. I've often heard people ask, "Does long-distance dating ever work?" I had two long-distance relationships over the years before Enrique, and obviously, neither one ended in marriage. But others have succeeded where I failed. In this chapter, I'll share some of what worked for them so you can decide whether you want to give it a try.

Fewer people ask whether "no-distance" relationships work. No-distance relationships, or what Dr. Kerry Cronin calls "pseudo-married couples," are the type of dating relationship where people's lives rapidly become very intertwined as they spend nearly all their time together. This certainly happens if they move in together, but even for Catholics who are striving for chastity and not living together before marriage, there's a danger of allowing someone who was a stranger a month or two ago to become practically the only person you talk to. This often happens in close-knit Catholic communities like small colleges and schools: everyone runs into the same people every day anyway, and dating simply decreases the distance between you and another person even more. This extreme closeness can cause issues for discernment, not to mention that the breakups from such no-distance relationships are absolutely brutal.

Of course, I'm not opposed to meeting a "pretty, good Catholic" in college; that's probably a much easier time to meet than any of the years after! But, as with everything, there are better ways and worse ways to do things. Here are some suggestions for overcoming the challenges of long-distance or no-distance relationships.

Long-Distance Dating: What Makes It Work?

The theme of my conversations with married couples who dated long-distance is that yes, long-distance relationships can work, but they take a lot of desire and effort on both sides. Here are the elements needed to make a long-distance relationship work well.

Communication and shared experiences

Of course, communication is important in all relationships, and historically, communication is harder over a distance and thus requires more effort. Today, though, long-distance communication has never been easier, with video calling technology and smartphones. And if you have romantic feelings for someone, there's an urge to spend time in conversation with him or her, even if it has to be through a screen.

But as humans with both bodies and souls, we also have a tendency to want to spend time physically in one another's presence. As I mentioned in Chapter Two, "Online Meeting, Not Online Dating" communication is not a relationship; it's just one aspect of a relationship.

If you're not having experiences together, it's easy to feel disconnected and even run out of things to talk about. Think about how easy it is to fall for someone who performed with you in a play or did mission work with you: those important experiences of working together are a powerful force that unites people. That glue is absent if you're in a totally long-distance relationship for any extended period of time.

Keep in mind that you always have a free choice whether or not to continue a relationship until you're actually married. If distance and lack of shared experiences or communication difficulties crop up early on in a relationship, you might decide it's just not practical to continue, and that's okay. You don't always have to have a moral or ideological reason to break up with someone. Sometimes, you have a situational reason. But if you prayerfully decide it's worthwhile to continue, you'll both have to put in the effort to keep up your connection.

I met Bernadette and Darren, a recently married couple, at a Young Catholic Professionals conference. They told me they had started dating in high school, continued as they attended different colleges many miles apart, and then finally married when they graduated. This is a rare genre of success story, so I asked them more about it. They mentioned that, when they first went off to college, communication was difficult. "We didn't see each other for the first two and a half months that we were in college. And I think we almost broke up in September of that year," Bernadette shared. "There were a lot of tough conversations those first couple months."

Things became much better once they prioritized seeing each other in person about once a month, either in their home town on breaks or by visiting each other's campuses. Between visits, they prioritized regular video calls. The summer before their senior year, when Darren had an internship that would keep him from spending the long break in their shared home town, he (and God) pulled strings to help Bernadette get work in the same place that summer, so they could live as neighbors and strengthen their relationship in-person for a few months. "That was a really good summer for us, I think, to grow together as a couple," said Bernadette, and in fact, it led to their engagement.

They both emphasized repeatedly that distance was still really hard and not something they would recommend to others. But once they could see themselves getting married in the future, making sacrifices for their relationship just made sense.

It helped that they had dated for the last year or so of high school before moving to a long-distance setup. They had shared experiences to draw from, and families and friends who knew each other to help keep them connected. I'll take this as an opportunity to re-emphasize what Dr. Greg Bottaro and others said in the chapter on online meeting: *dating happens in person*. If you have never met someone in person, you should not consider yourself in a committed relationship! Aside from the catfishing concern, it's just extremely difficult to build a meaningful relationship without shared experiences binding you together.

I won't say it's impossible, though; at least, I won't say that you *must* have the same home town or date for a year in person in order to build a good relationship that leads to a happy marriage. Kimmie and KJ are newlyweds who met at a national Singles for Christ conference. Their original meeting was in person, but brief, and their relationship developed mostly online. But it happened naturally, starting off as more of a friendship. "Snapchats became text messages, and then these long text messages became, 'Hey, let's go on a Skype call that lasted six hours,'" KJ shared. As their mutual feelings became clear, they wondered if they were becoming too committed without knowing when they would see each other again. So, they both took it to prayer, which leads nicely into the next point.

Prayer, with and for each other

Kimmie and KJ prayerfully discerned as they continued to get to know each other. In particular, when they had been talking for about three months, KJ met with a spiritual director and prayed in adoration before deciding to really pursue Kimmie. He shared an insight a friend gave him that's relevant for all discernment, not just long-distance dating: "When it comes to discernment, it's not between something good and bad. It's always good and good. Maybe there's a better choice, but it's between two good things. . . . You have to take action, and if it's something that wasn't meant to be, then it's okay, you'll get rerouted to what God wants." So, taking action to pursue Kimmie was the next step in discernment, and the rest was up to God.

Kimmie, meanwhile, was being pursued by a few different guys, but KJ stood out because of the substantive discussions they could have. They even told me they believed distance was a gift for them at first, because they could address the deeper topics that were important to them without worrying about the physical element of the relationship. "We're both words of affirmation people," shared Kimmie. From hearing them share their story, I think their relationship worked because their communication styles and love languages were similar, and because God clearly drew them together, something they were able to recognize through plenty of prayer.

As their relationship progressed over a distance, they would even go to Eucharistic adoration at the same time, albeit in different time zones: evening in Europe where KJ studied abroad and midday for Kimmie in the US. (Isn't that *adorable*?)

Removing the distance

At some point, if you are going to be married, at least one person has to move.

By most accounts, moving before marrying, preferably before getting engaged, is a very good idea, but this should be done with caution. Kimmie ended up moving to California for KJ once their relationship became serious enough, but she purposely chose a location a short distance from him where she could have her own community. This prevented her from getting too completely caught up in KJ's life and community (creating a no-distance relationship) and all the pressure on the relationship that might cause. Imagine moving to a new place where you only know your boyfriend or girlfriend, then slowly making friends among his or her friend group . . . while you settle into a new job, sign a lease, etc. Wouldn't it be extra hard to break up, even if you had a very good reason to do so?

On the other hand, remember what KJ's friend wisely pointed out to him: discernment requires taking action, and that includes spending enough time together to see whether you can build a happy, holy life together. That's nearly impossible without living in the same area.

Once you've seen a good amount of potential, moving could be worth it, whether it solidifies your relationship or reveals that you should part ways. One young man I know moved to a different state to be near his girlfriend so they could seriously consider engagement. Within a month of his move, their relationship came to an end. While they had visited each other often during their long-distance relationship, the greater amount of time spent together and more day-to-day interactions helped to clarify their discernment. Luckily, this man hadn't signed a long-term lease or gotten too embedded in the new city yet, so it was fairly easy to move again.

But for most people, the move would have been more risky. So consider all the risks before doing it. Are you moving to a place you'd be happy living, even if the relationship doesn't work out? Do you have any friends there, so you can be grounded in a faithful community, both during the relationship or if it ends? What will your housing situation be? Try to find a short-term lease or more casual rental like a family's basement apartment, so you aren't stuck if you need to move again. Consider the risks, reduce them where you can, but ultimately, be willing to take a little bit of risk if the relationship is worth it! Here's another area where God and your gut are necessary for making a decision in your unique situation.

It's easy for long-distance couples to chalk up personality difficulties to the distance, hoping or assuming that things will get better once they're in-person again. The only way to test that is to spend more time in-person, and see whether things really are better. In my two long-distance relationships, communication started to deteriorate badly, but I held on, thinking, "Distance is hard, but it will get better when he visits in X weeks." Usually, things felt a little better in person, because we could at least do something fun together. But in both relationships, I saw some "yellow flags" even during in-person visits: for instance, the men not making plans to spend quality time one-on-one, or conversation stalling too easily and too often. (Some silence is good, and even meaningful and romantic. But there's a difference between choosing to look silently into someone's eyes, and finding it difficult to keep up a conversation.)

In both cases, I pushed through the discomfort, not just for a day or a single visit, but for months, thinking I needed a better reason to end the relationship, or that it was all worth it because he checked all the boxes on my list. But God has shown me it's not always necessary to put myself through so much difficulty. Clinging to a difficult relationship will probably just lead to a difficult breakup or a difficult marriage. So spend enough time "in the flesh" to see whether the difficulties are easily overcome in the more natural setting of real life, or remain an issue.

By the way, healthy boundaries would have helped me discern better and quicker in both my long-distance relationships. A boundary in those cases would have looked like saying, "I would like to talk at least twice a week to keep up our relationship. If you don't have time to do that or don't want to, that's fine, but in that case, I don't think we should say that we're in an exclusive relationship." So often when I look back at prior relationships, I see that my misery was largely due to my own failure to communicate what I wanted! If I had spoken up, I could have either received what I wanted, or seen clearly that the relationship just wasn't going to work. (To learn more about this topic from a Christian perspective, see Dr. Henry Cloud's book *Boundaries*.)

If the issues are resolved, as you get more committed, talk more explicitly about when and how the long-distance phase might end. Consider what would be best for both of you and your future children, if you were to get married. Are there better Catholic schools in one place than another? Would you have some free childcare help if you lived near one of your families?

No-Distance Dating

I went to a small Catholic college. It was absolutely wonderful in many ways, from the curriculum to the culture, and lots of my classmates met their spouses there. But the student body fell prey to the high-pressure dating dynamic that often occurs in small, close-knit communities.

How do you know if you're in one of these small Catholic communities with a high-pressure dating environment? Here are some of the symptoms:

- If you're seen sitting next to someone of the opposite sex in Mass even once, everyone thinks you're dating.

- If you ask for or accept a date with someone, you are now "dating." (In other words, there's no such thing as just "a date;" it's either "in a relationship" or "nothing.")

- Also, "dating" means "probably getting married." A former philosophy professor of mine who specializes in family and relationships put it this way: "You go out for coffee one time, and everyone thinks you're in marriage prep!"

- It's normal to spend almost every waking hour with your boyfriend or girlfriend (e.g., eating all your meals together and taking all the same classes) . . . even if you only started dating a few days ago.

- And perhaps the most glaring sign: you fear that if you break up you'll destroy your whole friend group and never socially recover.

The pros of dating in a Catholic community are that, well, it's easy to meet fellow Catholics and get to know them, hopefully with a community around you that supports you in living virtuously. However, there are dangers with "no-distance dating."

Danger #1: Dating out of loneliness or an identity crisis

Often, no-distance relationships occur between people who have just moved or experienced a big transition. They may not have built a lot of good friendships yet, or may be trying hard to fit in or decide how to present themselves to others. If you've just arrived for your freshman year at university (or just moved to a new city), you might unwittingly dive into an intense no-distance relationship out of loneliness or simple excitement at being wanted, without discerning whether this person is actually good for you.

Also, college is often a time when people fall away from the Church, if they haven't already chosen to make the faith their own before that. Even if you don't fall away from the faith and you're dating a fellow Catholic, it might be very easy to change or ignore your physical boundaries, standards, goals, etc. when you're experiencing so much change. But if you do, it's likely you'll regret it later. For reasons like this, Dr. Mario Sacasa, in his course *Dating Well*, recommends not dating at all if you're in a time of major transition.

Developing and owning healthy boundaries will help a lot with all this. Your boundaries should at least include your spiritual and moral beliefs. If you don't know why you believe something, or why the Church teaches something, I recommend digging deeper by reading about it on the Catholic Answers website or some other reputable Catholic source. The Church has had over two thousand years to figure things out based on scripture and tradition, as well as a practical knowledge of human nature, so there's a deep explanation behind every teaching. Beyond your Catholic beliefs, you may need to set a few boundaries for yourself that aren't on a moral level, but are helpful for you personally.

It's important that you don't just unquestioningly adopt someone else's rules, because you need to really, firmly believe that your boundaries are good for you so that you will stick to them. But I suggest setting this boundary: "I will not get into an exclusive relationship (or won't date at all) until completing at least one semester," or "until I have at least two good, trustworthy Catholic friends in this new environment." In other words, consider setting dating aside temporarily until you have the time, space, and community you need to date with a clear mind and the right purpose.

Danger #2: Artificially high pressure

In a small community, dating can feel particularly high-pressure because of the tendency to go from zero to sixty immediately and become one of Cronin's "pseudo-married couples." After all, you see each other every day anyway, so to go from that to *dating* means being together even more. At first, this might be pure bliss: you get to go through every day with the person you like best! But over time, this constant contact can start to feel smothering.

When I first started dating someone in college, I recall feeling a bit stifled, not because of anything my new boyfriend was doing, but because the way I saw my pseudo-married peers behave made me feel that I *had* to hover around him whenever we had a break between classes, sit with him in the cafeteria three times a day, etc. I wanted a balance of dates, time with my friends, and time by myself, but I didn't know how to communicate that well to him.

If you're in a high-pressure environment, even a first date becomes an extremely big deal, because it almost automatically leads to a huge, life-changing commitment to spend all your time with your new love interest. Plus, everyone sees what's happening and talks about it. With too many voices talking about your relationship all around you, it can be hard to hear the voice of God or listen to your gut.

In a high pressure environment, even if you find something incompatible or morally suspect, or you just aren't happy in the relationship, you might feel embarrassed to break up because of what everyone else will say. Or you might worry about having to keep seeing the person you broke up with, because you're still in the small community, or else losing your friend group because you're avoiding the person. Not to mention, if your significant other is not only your best friend, but also your primary study buddy, ping-pong opponent, after-dinner conversationalist, and accountability partner, it's just more painful to break up. I've known couples who dated intensely, broke up, then got back together, sometimes more than once. It seemed as if their breakups were the result of "overdosing on each other." Or they broke up for good reasons, but fell back together because they had come to rely on each other so much they couldn't keep themselves apart.

So what can be done to take the pressure off, or to date well within a high-pressure environment?

First of all, of course, the brave thing to do is to break up with someone if you need to, and the sooner the better. The relationship will only become more high-pressure over time, especially if you get engaged. And, certainly, you should not marry someone just because breaking up with him or her would have rocked the social scene in undergrad. There's no way to completely rule out the possibility of this happening to you, unless you just decide not to date within your small community at all (which I don't recommend, because, again, this is actually a great place to meet good Catholics to date). At some point, the risks of heartbreak and social devastation are worth it for someone wonderful, and that's part of love.

But I think you can reduce this danger by having boundaries. Again, your exact boundaries will need to be your own, born of self-knowledge and the specifics of your situation. But I recommend two things:

- **Consider keeping quiet about your first few dates.** There's nothing wrong with preserving a little privacy so you have the mental space to discern well. Consider expressing how high-pressure the dating scene feels and asking, "Could we just quietly go out and see how it goes, and not tell anyone we're dating yet? If we end up going on several dates and deciding to pursue a relationship, we can share the news with everyone."

- **Plan specific dates; outside of those, go on with your life.** In order to pace yourself, have time and space to discern, and make sure you're keeping up a well-rounded life and other friendships, it's helpful to have a boundary on how much time you will spend together per week. I recommend coming up with a boundary like, "Let's have two or three one-on-one dates per week, but live our own lives the rest of the time." Technically, the word "date" indicates a date and time on the calendar when you plan to see someone. One of the problems with pseudo-married college couples is that they don't tend to actually go on dates much, but instead, just assume each other's constant presence. The spark in a relationship actually stays alive for longer if you have a little separation and look forward to seeing each other again. (It's also good practice for marriage. At least one of you will have to go to work or fulfill other duties instead of hanging out together all the time.)

When he asks you out to lunch . . . in the cafeteria. Dating on a student budget.

A note for gentlemen: if you're a broke college student who might not even have a car, taking a lady on nice dates might be hard to impossible, but you can still mimic the date mindset by planning the nicest things you can. Ask her to take a walk with you in a pretty part of town (free!). Invite her to grab meal-plan dinners to-go and head to a nice picnic spot to watch the sunset. And a night in with a movie and snacks is a classic! Just make sure it's clear you're not expecting a "Netflix and chill" (code words for a hookup).

A note for ladies: if your man is a broke college student, don't expect fancy restaurants and such. Money and atmosphere aren't the same as intentional pursuit. (You certainly don't want a man who goes into debt to take you on dates; it will only come back to bite you later.) Some of the best dates with my fiancé involved free or low-cost, spontaneous activities. (Once, he turned on classical music and we waltzed around his living room . . . *swoon*.) And, if you're more than a few dates in or are labeling yourselves boyfriend and girlfriend, it's completely fine for a woman to suggest a date idea yourself. But if you invite and it costs money, you offer to pay.

Danger #3: Missing out on important opportunities, unnecessarily

College and the young adult years are full of exciting opportunities. Not *everything* should be about pursuing a spouse. You might find yourself tempted to think that you shouldn't do X or Y because it would take you away from your boyfriend or girlfriend, but be very careful with that way of thinking.

At one point, I considered backing out of major travel plans, in part because I wanted more in-person time with my boyfriend. We had been long-distance for a bit because of his own travels, and I thought the difficulties I was sensing in our relationship would be resolved if I stayed in the US, where we would finally have a chance to date in person. (He never asked me to do this, for the record; it was just my own thought.) My mom gently convinced me to go through with the planned trip abroad, and I have long been grateful that I didn't miss that once-in-a-lifetime opportunity. For one thing, we ended up breaking up anyway, before my departure. But, even if we had continued the relationship, we could have used the tips earlier in this chapter to survive a few more months of long-distance dating, and had similar experiences of travel abroad to talk about when we were reunited. My desire to discern well by spending more time with him in person was a good one, but deciding to continue with my important, pre-arranged plans (made before we began dating) were important, too.

Striking the right balance here is hard, because at some point, it's important to make sacrifices for the person you love. Certainly, in marriage, that's crucial. But consider where you are in the relationship, how necessary it is for the health of the relationship for you to make this sacrifice, and whether you'll regret the sacrifice if the relationship doesn't become a marriage. In a healthy relationship, both people should desire to spend time together, but also be supportive of each other's goals and plans. So go to Europe (or to Colorado to train for the Olympics, or to Kalamazoo for the conference, whatever the opportunity is that you really want to take), but make a point to call or FaceTime regularly. If you really like him or her, and the opportunity is really important, you'll probably find a way to do both.

One last note: if your significant other is guilt-tripping you out of taking important opportunities so that you can spend time with him or her, this might be a red flag. Someone who loves you and who has a healthy respect for others' boundaries would instead say, "I'll really miss you if you decide to go, but it's okay. I'm excited for you and excited to hear all about it!" Remember, we're talking about dating here, not being married with kids. You don't have a duty to your boyfriend or girlfriend the way you would to a spouse and children.

The Non-Exclusive Stage in a No-Distance Environment: A Special Case

In an ideal world, the non-exclusive stage we discussed in Chapter Five would be essentially the same here: people wouldn't assume instant exclusivity, and it would be totally fine to date a few different people at the same time before settling into a relationship. However, this probably won't ever be the reality for a small, close-knit Catholic community. Once you're seen together or known to have gone on a date, the grapevine has a tendency to spread the word that you're "dating," and the word "dating" tends to imply a steady relationship in most people's minds. If you're a woman and word gets around that you're dating Kyle, Matt isn't likely to ask you out, because he thinks you're taken. And if you're a man and word gets around you're dating Gabby, Olivia is going to feel very strange about the fact that you're asking her out, too . . . and if word that you asked out Olivia gets back to Gabby, she might feel pretty strange as well. Pretty soon, you're in a socio-romantic mess.

Now, you could try to single-handedly change the dating culture on your campus by thoroughly communicating your method of dating and why you believe in a non-exclusive stage. But if you don't feel up to the task (and I don't blame you), you might have to adjust the non-exclusive stage by turning it into a lengthier friendship-in-groups stage, followed by a few dates where you're not seeing anyone else, but you're still taking it one date at a time (and possibly keeping the fact that you're going on dates to yourselves, as I suggested above). In the "real world," where you might meet people in totally different social groups and online, it's hard to get to know someone better without planning specific times to meet up, i.e. dates. But in a close-knit community, it's easier to get to know several people at once without going on dates, and it makes more sense to save one-on-one dates for when you're getting pretty comfortable with the idea of going exclusive.

So when you arrive on campus for a new year (or land a job as a Catholic camp counselor, or any other situation where you're surrounded by attractive single Catholics), challenge yourself to spend at least two to three months (or a semester, or even all of freshman year) getting to know everyone you might be interested in through group activities, and establishing plenty of same-sex friendships in different spheres while you're at it. Then you'll have a clearer idea of whom you're most interested in and other bonds to balance out the emotional bond of romantic interest, so that you slow down and stay clear-headed in a relationship. Plus, you'll have a good social safety net to fall back into if the relationship ends in a breakup.

There's another option, too. When I was in college, a professor gave us a talk encouraging us to wait to get into serious relationships until the second half of college, when we were past the major transition of starting college and closer to the possibility of marriage. But he also suggested *group* dates in the meantime, e.g., several men each asking a woman and going together to do something fun, the men paying and making sure the ladies have a nice time. I like this idea. Bowling or ice skating with several other couples is automatically less intimate and intense than a one-on-one dinner date, yet still preserves some of the fun of a date and exercises your dating etiquette.

Don't "Kiss and Tell": Dating Etiquette and Christian Charity

In the section on artificially high pressure, I suggested keeping quiet about your first few dates to reduce the pressure on your budding relationship. It's important to be careful what you say, not just for your own sake, but also for the sake of the other person. As Christians who are called to love others and will their good, we should be careful about what we say about others and avoid negative gossip.

The habit of curbing our tongues would go a long way toward changing the dating culture for the better. I asked the Catholic Dating subreddit about their experiences dating in tight-knit Catholic communities, and several men told me they were hesitant to ask someone out or to pursue too many women from the same community (even years apart) because they knew how much women talk to each other about their dates. As one user put it, "If you ask a girl out and she says no, then do not ask a girl in her orbit out. Even months later. . . . Girls talk, and in a small town it can be really bad. Once you ask one girl out, it's basically over."

This reminded me of something I learned long ago in a book called *365 Manners Kids Should Know*. Author Sheryl Eberly says that a girl should "keep it to herself" when she's said no to a date: "She especially shouldn't tell the next person he asks who does say yes." This is good manners (even for adults), because it prevents the next girl from feeling second-best and the guy from getting a reputation as someone who asks everyone out. Plus, when we ladies say no to a date, we always have some reason for it, so telling another girl that we declined a date (or ended a dating relationship) often implies something negative about him. The *Catechism of the Catholic Church* says that it is a sin of *calumny* to tell others about someone's faults unnecessarily (CCC 2477).

Try to avoid telling another woman that you've rejected a man she knows, and especially avoid telling her why. If you must share that you declined a date, it's usually sufficient to say something like, "He's great, just not for me." (Unless, of course, there is a very serious red flag that, out of charity, compels you to offer a warning.)

If you get into an exclusive relationship and then break up, of course, everyone around you will have to know something. But even then, you can be careful to whom you vent your feelings and consider how much you really need to say. Just as you wouldn't want your ex-boyfriend to talk bad about you to other single men, ruining your chances of dating them in the future, don't talk bad about him to single women who might be his future prospects.

When I was dating non-exclusively, it felt particularly important to me not to "name names," in case a friend was also going out with the same guy, or might in the future. When a dating connection ended, I wanted that man to be able to ask out anyone he wanted with a fresh start. And I wanted this for my dates because I wanted it for myself. This didn't mean I couldn't talk about my dating life at all—that would be impossible for any woman! Instead, I made up code names for my dates and tried to share the basics without too many identifying details. Enrique was "Medical Man" (because he was working on prerequisites for nursing school) until he was the only one I was seeing.

I've been speaking primarily to women here as the ones who are more known for talking in detail about everything. Of course, all of this goes for men too. Don't "kiss and tell" or even "have a conversation and tell"! Instead, have some boundaries around your own words, for yourself and for the sake of the people you date.

7

. . . .

The Exclusive Stage

Dealbreakers and Discernment

ong ago, I saw a post on Tumblr that said, "Dating is scary because you're either going to break up or get married." It's true. The real drama begins in the exclusive stage, when you decide whether to marry this person, or break up and start all over.

In the non-exclusive stage, you were taking it one date at a time, considering whether you wanted to go on one more date and whether you could see potential for a more serious relationship. Marriage was still the ultimate goal, but a more remote one. In the exclusive stage, you're in that more serious relationship, so marriage is a much more proximate goal. You're opening up more, becoming vulnerable to having your heart broken. That's scary—but also exciting!

Remember the checklist I had you throw out back in Chapter One? It's finally time to pick it up again, but in a modified form. As you become exclusive and start using the boyfriend/girlfriend labels, it is important to have standards to guide your discernment and to start paying more attention to any strong preferences you may have. Like any loving parent, God likes to fulfill our desires whenever it's good for us, so our deep, persistent, good desires can be helpful road signs pointing us in the right direction.

This chapter will be more serious and mention some heavier themes that haven't come up yet. That's necessary, because your relationship is becoming more serious and there's heavy stuff you'll have to deal with, no matter whom you're dating. But don't forget to enjoy this stage, too. Sometimes we present "dating for marriage" and "dating for fun" as opposites, but there's no reason they should be. If you're not still enjoying your relationship as you "get serious," something is seriously wrong. More on that below.

How to Make It Official

This phase starts when you have a conversation and decide to enter this phase. I do not recommend assuming you're in this phase when you haven't explicitly said so. Matchmaker Cristina Pineda recommends that the man bring up the topic of exclusivity. She also assures women that men *will* do so if they're really interested, and if the relationship has remained chaste. "At some point, men are driven by that end goal of wanting to sleep with a woman," Pineda told me in an interview. "Often women will ask me, 'Well, what if he doesn't say anything?' You just have to *not* sleep together, and then this will take its natural course, because the man will want to lock you down for himself."

This sounds blunt, but think about what Pineda is really saying here. Biological instincts are a real thing, created by God for good reasons. If a woman doesn't give herself completely away from the start, a man who's interested in her will continue to pursue her and ask for the next level of commitment, moving toward marriage and the appropriate time for sexual intimacy.

But what exactly should a man say when he asks for exclusivity? We live in a world of confusion, and people use words to mean different things. The words "boyfriend" and "girlfriend" are two of my least favorite in the world, in part because their meanings are so broad. In our culture, they can mean anything from someone with whom you occasionally have dinner to someone with whom you share a bank account and child. Even among Catholics, "boyfriend" and "girlfriend" might imply slightly different things. (Someone might want a girlfriend even though he's definitely not planning to marry within the next few years, while his girlfriend might assume a proposal will follow in six months.)

It's important to say everything aloud. Talk about what it means to be boyfriend and girlfriend (or "exclusive" or "official" or whatever words you choose to use). Define the basic terms of your relationship.

When Enrique asked me to be his girlfriend, I asked him what that meant to him, and we agreed that it meant we were actively discerning marriage with each other and no one else. That would include discussing more serious topics that we hadn't addressed yet. We made a point of meeting each other's families within a few weeks after that, because that was important to both of us.

Similarly, Amanda and Chris from the chapter on online meeting had a conversation early on about what being "official" meant to them and what their boundaries were. "The biggest thing was confirming that we both had the intention of pursuing marriage. And then throughout our relationship, it was a natural progression: 'I want you to meet my family, and I want you to meet my friends, and we're going to put the time and effort into actually discerning whether our lives are compatible,'" said Amanda.

Take a page from their book and mine (pun intended, because we need some "dad jokes" in a book about dating): define your terms, and make sure both of you have the same goal of considering marriage so that you're clear on how far down the road you'd like to go if you keep getting green lights.

Know What You're Looking For: Three Dealbreakers

You've probably heard the advice that you need to "know what you're looking for" in a spouse. In the chapter "You Don't Have a Type," I essentially told you that you don't need a checklist to start dating, because so often what we're looking for isn't actually what's best for us. But there are a few things that everyone should be looking for in a spouse and that you should probably see in a person *before* deciding to go "official." You can think of these things as *standards*—things that must be present—or their opposites as *dealbreakers*—things that must be absent. These are the bare minimum criteria; we'll talk about preferences in a moment.

Pineda says that, in her experience working with clients for over a decade, there are three important dealbreakers every couple must align on: wanting to get married, wanting to have children, and religious compatibility. Let's consider each one as it applies to a Catholic context.

Desire to get married

It's easy to assume that any Catholic or Christian who's interested in dating is interested in marriage. But a friend of mine who's been on the dating scene for a long time cautioned me to ask what a man is looking for by about the fourth date. She had run into too many men who didn't want marriage and were dating, I guess, for companionship or in hopes of getting sex without marriage eventually, even if they were religious. Again, we live in a world of confusion and differing expectations. If it doesn't come up organically during the first few dates, ask about it: "Are you hoping to get married if you find the right person?" or "Is marriage an important goal for you?"

I will say, though, I think people who are dating for marriage tend to mention that or hint at it within the first few dates. A conspicuous lack of saying *anything* about marriage, even in the abstract, for example, "I hope to travel abroad with my spouse someday," might imply that marriage isn't a major goal right now. As always, don't assume either way, but ask and communicate.

Another angle that applies particularly to devout Catholics: check on your date's "discernment status" (so to speak) before getting serious. If you want to get on the fast train to marriage because you believe it's God's will for you, and your date is still hovering between marriage and a celibate vocation, this can cause enormous heartbreak later. Again, if it doesn't come up organically after a month or two of non-exclusive dating, ask your date, "Have you ever considered religious life/priesthood?" and see how the conversation unfolds.

Lastly, besides simply *wanting* to get married, both parties must be capable of a valid marriage in the Catholic Church. Some things that are obstacles to a valid marriage include (but are not limited to):

- Having a living spouse, even if divorced, unless the Catholic Church has annulled the previous marriage.

- Having previously taken vows of religious life or been ordained a priest, unless those vows have been dispensed.

- Being impotent. (Infertility is not an obstacle, but impotence is.)

- Having a mental condition that prevents the person from fully understanding and fulfilling the vows of marriage.

- Not knowing what marriage really is (a faithful, lifelong union of a man and a woman who are open to having children—see below).

- Being forced or pressured into the marriage.

- Being too closely related to each other.

If you are cousins with your date, secretly a priest, or have a mysterious rich uncle who says you have to get married by age twenty-one in order to inherit the estate, please inform your date up front.

Openness to children

The Church teaches that in order to marry validly, the couple must be open to having any children God may give them. I'm not qualified to go into all the nuances of what "open to children" means, but here's a quick and simple refresher. People who know they are infertile, whether due to age or health issues, can still have a valid sacramental marriage (and they are not obligated to seek adoption). But couples who are presumed fertile may not enter marriage with the *intention* of never having children. Because sex, marriage, and babies are all fundamentally connected in God's plan and the Church's teaching, someone who just doesn't want kids shouldn't be getting married, and therefore shouldn't be getting into a serious dating relationship.

You might already know all this, but again, don't assume that anyone who says they're Catholic or longs for marriage automatically desires children. If something about "my future kids" hasn't organically come up, ask your potential boyfriend or girlfriend about his or her desires for a future family. I don't recommend asking, "How many kids do you want?" on a first date (that's a little intimidating), but something like, "Do you hope to have kids someday?" is totally appropriate when you're approaching the exclusivity conversation. (And lest you think that wanting children is pretty universal, a quick search for "child free" will reveal a huge and growing swath of young people who are adamantly opposed to having kids.)

What if *you* want to be married but don't want children? I recommend prayerfully exploring whether there's a wound or excessive fear there, maybe with a counselor. Sometimes, friends of mine have expressed fear or lack of desire for children if they don't have a lot of experience with children. If that's your case, consider looking for opportunities to spend time with kids, maybe by assisting with Sunday school classes at your parish or babysitting for friends who are parents. Kids are challenging, but they are also extraordinarily cute and absolutely hilarious. Get to know some before you decide not to have any!

But if you discern that you really shouldn't have children for some reason, it's likely God isn't leading you to marriage. At least, you most definitely shouldn't discern marriage with someone who wants children. I've heard it said that there's no compromise between having a child and not having a child. Not sharing a desire for children should be an absolute dealbreaker, for all kinds of moral, spiritual, and practical reasons.

Dating as a Single Parent, or with an Annulment in Your Past

Dating is extra difficult for those who were previously married and/or have children. One woman I met through my singles' ministry tended to start conversations with, "I'm divorced and annulled, and I have kids." No takers, sadly! Another woman worried she would be rejected solely because of her annulment.

I asked Cristina Pineda for advice. Of dating with children, she recommended mentioning that you have children on the first date. She also emphasized the importance of being extra careful who you date, running a background check and searching sex offender registries, and never leaving your kids alone with your boyfriend or girlfriend. And be careful about letting your children get very attached to him or her, in case the relationship ends. Pineda suggests introducing your children to your significant other "when the relationship is serious and moving toward engagement." On the other hand, you may want to do it sooner to see how they get along, but consider introducing him or her as "a friend" and avoiding overtly couple-like behavior.

Pineda also says that people without children should be open to dating a single parent, but be aware that they are also discerning the possibility of becoming a parent figure. I know someone who had no children herself when she married a widower with several school-age kids. She mentioned that it would have been nice to "just change diapers for a while," and yet, it was also nice not to have to. The role of step-parent is a unique calling.

As for annulments, Pineda says it's probably good to mention it if you go on multiple dates, but there's no need to share details about why your previous marriage was annulled: "You need to have a simple explanation that makes it clear you're not still hung up on that relationship." If they press you for info, you can simply say that you'll share more if your relationship progresses.

One thing I notice in her responses: you probably don't need to share about your annulment or even your children *before* a first date. You have a personality outside those things. So it's okay to ask questions and chat about common interests first, rather than *leading* with a potentially difficult fact about yourself. Share soon enough, but not too soon.

Religiously compatible

A whole chapter is coming up on whether you should date a non-Catholic or even a different "type" of Catholic. For now, I'll just say that if you're reading this book you probably would ideally hope to marry a fellow Catholic, even if you're open to other options. Hang onto that hope! At minimum, you probably hope to have a sacramental marriage, which can only happen between two baptized persons. Hang onto that hope too!

I personally believe that you shouldn't get engaged to someone unless you are "equally yoked," which typically means that you are both Catholic and of approximately equal devotion or commitment to your faith. But that doesn't necessarily mean you should restrict *dating* only to people who already meet this criterion. If you are firm in your faith yourself, it might be sufficient for religious compatibility at this stage that your date is committed to seeking truth, is exploring Catholicism, and isn't doing any harm to your faith. After all, several of the couples I interviewed for this book (Kayla and Rudy from Chapter Two, Bernadette and Darren from Chapter Six) and many others have dated non-Catholics who ended up converting, at least in part through the relationship. This is something to be done with caution. Again, more on that in another chapter.

Discerning Marriage, More Concretely

So, you've had the conversation, you have a new boyfriend or girlfriend. Now what? What does discerning marriage look like in the day-to-day, and how do you know whether he or she is "the one" for you?

There's no one perfect formula here, because discerning marriage with a unique person is going to be a unique experience. In fact, I asked a Catholic psychologist, Dr. Bryan Violette (who works with the CatholicPsych Institute), what two people should have in common to build a happy, holy marriage, and he said that this varies by the couple. "How many love stories are there? As many as there are couples. So, you see couples that are exactly alike, right? They have the same temperament, and that works for them. And then you have some where there's a lot more complementarity, and they're two very different people," said Violette. "What might be difficult for me may not be difficult for you."

But, keeping that in mind, Violette and others can still offer some helpful tips. Based on their advice, here are some suggested red, yellow, and green flags to look for as you date more seriously.

Red and Yellow Flags

As Dr. Violette indicated, some things that are yellow flags (difficulties to be managed) for one couple might be red flags (or dealbreakers) for another. But seeing too many of these red or yellow flags probably means this relationship just isn't right for you.

He/she is unaware of flaws or unable to work on them

Dr. Violette told me, "We all have psychological issues, we all have sins, we all succumb to temptations. So the red flag is when someone can't change." He also said to consider to what extent the issue is affecting your relationship. (Inability to have a respectful disagreement—either fleeing from conflict or becoming excessively angry, etc.—will probably affect your relationship more than, say, over-indulging in dessert now and then, though both are worth working on.) Of course, if you want a spouse who's aware of his or her flaws and working on them, you need to have a similar desire for growth. "A good working definition of mental health is, 'How flexible are you?'" said Violette.

You are too different from each other in important areas

"This expression 'opposites attract' is not true. Opposites do not attract," says Dr. Mario Sacasa in his course *Dating Well*. "You cannot be the exact opposite of your boyfriend on major items like faith, how many kids you want to have, or how you want to spend your money, and expect the relationship to work." We already talked about being religiously compatible and open to children, but those issues bear emphasizing again.

The third item Dr. Sacasa mentions, money, is also an important topic to discuss with your boyfriend or girlfriend as the relationship progresses. Many divorces stem from arguments over money and a perception that the other spouse is either spending too much on the wrong things or not earning enough. Talk about your spending tendencies honestly. Are you more of a spender or a saver? Do you prefer to buy low-cost items more often, or spend more on something long-lasting? When do you think it's okay to take on debt? Also, consider what lifestyle you're each accustomed to. I've seen a relationship experience tension because one person was more well-off and showed affection through lavish gift-giving, while the other was used to a thriftier lifestyle and felt uncomfortable with the gifts.

You are too similar to each other . . . supposedly

In the book *Boundaries*, Dr. Henry Cloud mentions that if two people never disagree on anything, at least one of them probably has poor boundaries. Two people are always going to have differences, so at least one of them must be hiding real opinions or needs out of a fear of starting an argument or being rejected. It's good to have lots of overlap in key areas like the three important ones just mentioned above, as well as love language, what you like to do for fun, and even eating habits. As Fr. T. G. Morrow says in his book *Christian Dating in a Godless World*, "Friendship is the most important natural ingredient for a good marriage. Since friendship is based on common interests, similarities are very important."

But differences should also be allowed to come out, and those can be a strength too. I really appreciate how open, communicative, and physically affectionate Enrique is, despite those not being my strongest points, because he helps me grow in those areas. But there's enough overlap between us for the relationship to work smoothly. For instance, physical affection is his primary love language, but quality time—my primary love language—is also a major one for him. When it comes to what we like to do for fun, he's a fan of roller coasters while I scream compulsively if he lifts me six inches off the ground. But we share an interest in dancing and both love a relaxed Sunday afternoon with our families. We're different and not afraid to express those differences, but we aren't polar opposites.

You or others around you see signs of abuse

I've spoken with people who have suffered emotional, physical, or sexual abuse in relationships. There's a common trait: it's *very* hard to recognize abuse while it's happening to you, especially if you're unfamiliar with it or haven't been in a relationship before. Be informed about the warning signs of abuse, and be open with trustworthy friends and family about what's going on in your relationship, so others can help spot the signs if they arise.

According to the CatholicPsych blog, "How to Spot Emotional Abuse," if your partner is consistently very moody, isolates you from friends and family, or uses extreme sarcasm and hypercriticism rather than engaging in respectful disagreement, these are some signs of emotional abuse. The feeling of "walking on eggshells" is also common among victims of emotional abuse, who feel a constant need to avoid angering the abusive person.

Physical and sexual abuse might sound more straightforward, but it's still not always easy to spot the warning signs. I spoke with someone who experienced a disastrous, abusive marriage that even included rape. Before the wedding, her then-boyfriend ignored or argued with her physical boundaries and requests . . . but switched back to being nice whenever she pulled away, making her believe he had changed. This pattern showed how, ultimately, he wanted to *control* her, rather than love her. This is a classic sign of abuse.

If you state a reasonable boundary, and your boyfriend or girlfriend ignores it, mocks it, fights with you about it, or tries to guilt-trip you into thinking you should change it, that's a major red flag. There's a loving, respectful way to disagree, ask questions, and even give feedback while respecting someone's free will. But when someone you're dating tries to control you, whether through force or manipulation, walk away, permanently.

On a related note, I came across a Reddit post in which a woman shared that her boyfriend was a mostly nice guy, but would occasionally become enraged, use insults and profanity toward her, accuse her of doing wrong when she hadn't, and then refuse to talk to her until she apologized. Of course, these are all enormous violations of charity *and* indicators of abuse. But he had convinced her to stay around and put up with his bad behavior by saying that she needed to submit to him, as practice for marriage.

St. Paul does say that wives should be subject to their husbands (Ephesians 5), but sometimes men twist this to mean that they should have *power* over their wives—and even girlfriends. That is simply not true. Remember that Paul also calls husbands to be Christlike and willing to lay down their lives for their wives! And Christ doesn't insult, manipulate, or force people into doing anything. If you have a boyfriend (or girlfriend) who selectively leverages scripture as an excuse for bad behavior, you do *not* have a good Catholic boyfriend (or girlfriend).

Submission is a big, nuanced topic, but it ultimately means something more like respect, trust, and willingness to listen—*not* putting up with mistreatment. And being the head of the family means exercising servant leadership and looking out for everyone's welfare—not being a moody dictator. Most of all, wifely submission does not mean you have to stay with someone when you're not even his wife! As another Reddit user put it, "If this is how he acts now, how do you think he'll act if you commit to him (in marriage)?"

He or she stops pursuing or prioritizing you

In all three of my serious relationships before Enrique, there came a point where my then-boyfriends stopped actively pursuing me. It showed up as less proactive communication, fewer planned one-on-one dates, consistently prioritizing time with other friends over time with me (some of this is healthy, but too much is not), or just a general stalling of progress. Conversations remained at the same level rather than deepening and allowing us to get to know each other better. Each time, I held on anyway and thought, "Things will get better over time," or "This relationship seems less fun now, but maybe that's normal after you're through the honeymoon phase." But each time, this stagnation was followed by the men breaking up with me.

I say this with no bitterness at all toward them, because they all had good reasons for ending the relationship, and I'm happily engaged to Enrique now. But I share it because I think a lack of pursuit from the man's side is a yellow flag that indicates something isn't going well with the relationship, and it's okay for a woman to speak up and ask, "Is everything okay between us? How do you think our relationship is going?"

It goes the other way too, of course. Though ideally the man should be doing more of the pursuing throughout the relationship, a woman will normally reciprocate and prioritize the relationship pretty highly if she's falling in love. If you get to a point where you feel like you're doing all the work to hold the relationship together, something is not right. Maybe it can be resolved, or maybe it's time to move on. As always, the first step is to communicate about the issue. You shouldn't really be through with the honeymoon phase until at least, well, your actual honeymoon.

Green Flags

Once again, there's no perfect formula for discerning marriage with a unique person. But if these green flags are present in your relationship, it's probably healthy and going well.

You see personal growth in yourself

Dr. Sacasa and others say that one of the signs of a healthy relationship is that you grow and improve within it, rather than being dragged down. I experienced a lot of emotional healing and spiritual growth during just the first few months of dating Enrique, and I continue to change for the better with him now, in engagement. I also see growth in him over time.

Sometimes, forming a close relationship can trigger people to realize their wounds and issues, and then they respond by pulling away to work on those things. Sometimes, that's a good idea, if the issues are affecting the relationship too much, or the relationship is making the issues worse. But it's not always necessary. My friend Anne, who's a therapist, often says, "We are healed in relationship," whether it's a relationship with a professional therapist, a friend, family, or a significant other (or preferably, a combination of these, because we all need a well-rounded community).

You like how you act around the person

One of my dad's wise dating tips comes in the form of a question: "Do you like who you are around him/her?" When we talked about it, my dad clarified that he doesn't just mean, "Does this person make me a better person?" (although that's good to consider too), but also, "Do I *like myself* around this person? Does this person bring out aspects of myself that I enjoy?" If someone's personality naturally brings out all or nearly all the good sides of yours, instead of triggering your bad tendencies, that's a good sign. Enrique and I particularly appreciate that we can bring out each other's intellectual side and discuss philosophical topics, but we can also laugh together at the silliest things.

You like how you feel around the person

On her podcast, Christian author and dating influencer Kait Warman encourages people, particularly women, to pay attention to how they're feeling in their bodies around someone. I've sometimes experienced feeling sick to my stomach or hesitant to stand or walk close to a man on a date (in a way that I knew wasn't just nerves, because I'm not usually *that* nervous on a date). Sometimes, when I was trying to convince myself that a failing relationship was fine, my body and brain would try to tell me the truth by becoming very depressed or anxious. Once, I had a dream that the guy I was dating was roller-skating too fast, and I couldn't keep up or understand where he was going . . . in hindsight, definitely symbolic of how I felt I was struggling to keep his attention! Not every feeling, dream, or depressive episode is caused by your romantic relationship, but if you're constantly anxious, irritated, sad, nauseated, or tired around someone, it's worth paying attention to that as one data point in the larger picture. Similarly, if you get excited and happy around someone, that's one good data point in the larger picture.

You can share your whole self with him/her

When we hear that marriage is a "total gift of self," we often think of sexual intimacy, the total gift of the body and fertility to the other person. But a total gift of self extends beyond the body. Dr. Violette emphasized to me that couples need to be able to share their whole selves, including the less-pleasant aspects of their souls, with each other. "You want to unscrew the bolts in your chest and open that up and share these pieces that you don't want to show anyone else and have them say, 'I accept you and I love you anyway,'" he said. You probably shouldn't share all those things right away, but by the time you promise to marry someone (remember Cristina Pineda's three columns of conversation topics?) you should be able to share everything important about yourself and know that you are still loved.

I think a good litmus test for whether you can share your whole self with someone, one that is appropriate even earlier in the relationship, is this: can you comfortably introduce your boyfriend or girlfriend to every significant friend, family member, or group in your life? In one past relationship, I felt awkward talking with my then-boyfriend about some of my interests and even a lay Catholic movement called Communion and Liberation I'm involved in because I felt that he might not like it. Maybe he actually would have, given the chance

. . . but I wasn't brave enough to risk it. With Enrique, I very quickly felt comfortable sharing all my interests, from Communion and Liberation to *Pride and Prejudice*. He gets along with my family and friends, all of whom have had an influence on my personality over the years. So, I can see that he gets along with all of me. I recommend being brave and sharing all your interests, passions, and important friendships with your significant other pretty early, as a way to start learning whether you can trust him or her with those more personal and less-pleasant aspects of yourself.

Your major goals and desires align

Beyond the shared desire to marry and have children, which is an absolute necessity, you might have other strong and long-cherished desires for your life that should align with the other person's. This is just practical. If you want to have a happy life together, you'll need a shared vision of what "happy" looks like.

In their book *Boundaries in Dating*, Dr. Henry Cloud and Dr. John Townsend give the example of a person who feels called to long-term international mission work, and points out that this person won't be a good fit for someone who doesn't share that calling and goal. I have heard of whole families moving across the globe to be missionaries together, but that's a unique calling that both spouses must share.

My experience is more mundane, but over the years I was repeatedly confirmed in a deep desire to continue living near my family, with the hope that my children would grow up near all their grandparents, as I did. I didn't make "must be from Nashville" a dealbreaker for a first date, of course, but I did start to notice whether the men I met had family in the area and seemed interested in sticking around. On our first date, I found out that Enrique had followed his family to Tennessee from California because living near them was a high priority for him. It was another "green flag" that I should continue getting to know him; we shared one major piece of our vision for life.

If your hope is to be a full-time homemaker, and your boyfriend is just beginning a career as an artist, you might need to have an honest conversation about your future income and living situation. Could you both take on steady part-time jobs as a compromise until the art career is off the ground, or are you just not a fit for each other? If you hope to have a wife who's a full-time homemaker, and your girlfriend is a successful lawyer who loves her work, that will take an honest conversation too. (And go into that conversation with many prayers to the Holy Spirit; gender roles and women's careers can be sensitive topics.) It's important that both of you are asking God and yourselves, "What's best for the common good of our future family?"

A controversial question: Should mothers work outside the home?

I can't fully answer this big question here, but I'll offer a few clues. Firstly, some say that the Church teaches that women should not work outside the home, or at least shouldn't do so without grave necessity. I have never been able to find such a thing in any magisterial document. The closest thing I can find is *Rerum Novarum*, in which Pope Leo XIII writes on workers' rights, but he merely says that women (and children!) in the workplace should be given proper accommodations, rather than automatically being expected to do the same type and amount of work as men. Besides, throughout most of history, women actually *had* to work to make ends meet. The "fifties housewife" life was pretty much only a reality in the fifties, a time of remarkable wealth and economic advantages for Americans after World War II . . . not particularly traditional or tied to Christianity.

However, the Church also teaches that parents are the primary educators of their children, and "educators" doesn't primarily refer to academic teaching, but overall rearing and formation. It seems clear that to be the primary formators of your children, you'll need to spend a good amount of time with them day-to-day. Plus, scientific studies have shown that, for children under age three, all-day daycare rather than parental care at home can cause increased cortisol (stress hormone) levels that lead to behavioral and mental health issues—even an increased chance of criminal activity—years down the road. I don't say this to make anyone feel scared or guilty (if you went to daycare as a child, you can still turn out just fine!), but it seems that both faith and science agree: if children can possibly be cared for at home by a parent through the toddler years, they will probably experience positive effects on their mental health and morality. (Learn more at the Institute for Family Studies and criticalscience.medium.com.)

You trust this person to make good decisions, with God's help

Trust can be hard, even when you know someone well, because we all like control. It's hard to let go and let someone else make choices without our input. But in marriage, your spouse will frequently have to make decisions on his or her own. You should talk about big decisions together whenever possible, but what if your spouse is alone with the kids and needs to make a split-second decision about discipline? What if you're the victim of a terrible accident, and your spouse is the one making choices about what the doctors will do for you? For that matter, would you trust this person with your children if you passed away?

These are big, terrifying questions that are hard to answer with a firm "yes" when you haven't already been through decades of life together. But you can start to detect the presence or absence of trustworthiness in your potential spouse in smaller ways. Does he or she follow through on promises to meet up at a particular time, or constantly flake on plans? Does he or she lie about anything, or tell the truth even when it's unpleasant to do so? Does he or she lose jobs, money, or relationships because of untrustworthy behavior toward others, or is he or she generally liked and respected? Does he or she make appropriate sacrifices for you and truly desire your good?

Lately, I've been meditating on how Our Lady, who was so close to God herself, was able to trust St. Joseph when he said they needed to flee to Egypt with the child Jesus. He received the message from an angel telling them to go, and Mary had to trust that Joseph was really hearing the voice of the Lord. Is your love interest close to the Lord and conversing with Him daily? If you trust that he or she listens to God, trusting him or her becomes much easier.

Trust takes some time and practice to build. For our third date, I let Enrique plan the date as a surprise for me, giving me just enough information so I would know how warmly to dress. It was a wonderful date, and from then on, I've been able to trust him with bigger and bigger things, because I've seen that trusting him so far has turned out very well. The number one reason I know I can trust him with the rest of my life and my future children is his personal, conversational relationship with God and his devotion to the Church and the sacraments.

A Few More Tips for the Exclusive Stage

This chapter has been pretty introspective, focusing on big questions that will take the entire exclusive stage to answer. I'll close with two more tips that are more immediately actionable and make the exclusive stage more enjoyable. Your relationship shouldn't just be heavy conversations for months on end!

Continue *actually* dating

In my past experience, whenever I'd gotten "official" with someone, we tended to get out of the habit of planning official dates. He'd rarely if ever actually ask me out anymore; instead, the majority of our time together would happen by spur-of-the-moment hanging out at each other's houses and showing up together to group social events. Some of this is good and natural. But it's easy to lose the intentionality in your relationship and start taking each other for granted. For me, this caused the flame of romance to flicker a bit because I didn't feel as if I was being pursued in the same way. To this day, even though we have plenty of "casual time" together, Enrique still regularly plans thoughtful, fun dates. (Once, during our engagement, he made a date out of apartment hunting. Even chores can become dates if you add ice cream.)

I recommend continuing to go on real dates at least sometimes. Gentlemen, continue to pursue her, and ladies, make it clear that you appreciate his thoughtfulness and generosity. Don't take each other's time and attention for granted.

This is easier if you keep up the rest of your interests and friendships, allowing some natural separation. If you usually go to Tuesday night Bible study (or softball or pottery class) and your significant other asks you to hang out on Tuesday, say that you have prior plans and suggest an alternate day. It's probably good to see each other several times a week at this stage if possible, but it doesn't have to be every day. Give yourselves some space to look forward to the next time you'll see each other. Whether or not you're in a small, close-knit community, there's the temptation to collapse into a no-distance relationship, and it's best to avoid that.

Remember that you're not married

Even though a milestone has been achieved by your committing to focus on this person right now, it's a milestone that is not marked by a ring, a liturgy, or the Code of Canon Law. In the eyes of God and the Church—that is, in *reality*—you are still just two separate people, getting to know each other. Remember that you're not married.

Now, you might be thinking, "Yes, I know, that means we shouldn't have sex." Correct, chastity might become more difficult as time goes on, and it's still extremely important. But I'm pointing to more than that.

If we've been unchaste, do we need to break up?

Chastity is hard, especially when you've found someone you connect with intellectually, emotionally, and spiritually as well as finding him or her physically attractive. If you fall in this area, first of all, remember that this is not unusual. Sexual sin is bad, but Jesus died precisely because all of us do a lot of bad things that need forgiving. You're not irredeemable, and your relationship might not be either; if you can both go to confession, have an honest conversation about what led to your fall, and commit to avoiding that situation going forward, you might actually come out with a better, more chaste relationship. (See Fr. Mike Schmitz's video "Avoiding Impurity" for some thoughts on this and how to avoid the temptation going forward.)

From time to time, I've encountered Catholic dating couples who seem to forget that they aren't duty-bound to "make it work." A relationship becomes difficult and draining, but one partner keeps clinging anyway. Sometimes, they cling out of a sense of scarcity: "Will I ever find anyone else this good?" Or, they think that this amount of hardship is normal: "Relationships take work. I shouldn't break up with him/her just because she/he isn't perfect." But how much work is too much?

Dr. Mario Sacasa addresses this point in his course *Dating Well*. Sacasa says, "Everyone says that relationships take work, and while that is absolutely true, that doesn't mean that relationships should be laborious all the time." He offers the example of his son, who is a natural at playing baseball, but still works hard at practice, too. "He deeply enjoys playing the game, so he is more motivated to play with his friends and practice harder. He is putting in the work, but it's all within this feeling of ease and comfort," says Sacasa. "There should be this kind of ease and genuine connection in a relationship."

Only you can decide whether or not the difficulties you face are acceptable to you and whether there's enough ease and comfort to balance out the things you must labor through together. But I think the level of "making it work" should be proportional to the stage of the relationship you're in. If you're already married, you'll need to "make it work" (unless, of course, there's a grave enough problem that the Church would allow you to live separately, such as abuse). If you're just boyfriend and girlfriend and you've had difficulties almost from the beginning, you're under no obligation to "make it work." These difficulties might be red flags to you, even if they're yellow flags to someone else, and that's okay. There are more pretty, good Catholics out there than you realize, and a good relationship will give you more peace and joy (which are fruits of the Holy Spirit!) than pain and stress.

To sum up: if you want a happy, holy marriage, look at the person you're considering marrying and see whether you are happy and holy (or at least growing in holiness) with him or her right now. The best predictor of the future is the past.

8

. . . .

Dating Outside Your Tribe

Should I Date a Non-Catholic or a Different Type of Catholic?

"What do you think about dating Protestants?" a friend asked me, as we ate our pad Thai. She's a very devout Catholic, exceptionally pretty and well-dressed, loving and generous. Although she says she's shy on the inside, she comes across chatty and fun, and even feisty when the situation calls for it. Number one on the list of things she's willing to be feisty about: her Catholic beliefs. When her Protestant coworkers here in the Bible belt confront her about them, she has an answer ready.

But she's at her wit's end trying to find a Catholic spouse, hence her question. Maybe you are too. Maybe, like the woman I mentioned in Chapter Three, you find that the Catholics you meet are boring or awkward, and non-Catholics are more interesting. Maybe, like Kayla from Chapter Two, you're always running into the same people in the Catholic "bubble" and looking to branch out. Or maybe, you happen to "just meet" someone as you live your well-rounded life . . . and that someone is attractive, smart, kind, funny—and not Catholic. Should you date him or her anyway?

My initial answer to my friend was another question: "Do you want to *marry* a Protestant?" Because dating is ultimately for considering marriage, it makes sense to consider whether you should marry a non-Catholic, then work backward to dating.

If you're reading this book, you probably ideally want to marry a fellow Catholic, a devout one who will help you grow closer to God and be prepared for heaven. That's a good and realistic standard that I think you should cling to. It's also scriptural: St. Paul says, "Do not be mismatched with unbelievers" (2 Corinthians 6:14). In some translations, the verse says, "Do not be unequally yoked with unbelievers." When we look for a life partner, we should look for someone to be "equally yoked" with on the journey to heaven. But does that mean you should only date Catholics? Is it bad to "flirt to convert" or "missionary date," that is, date someone who doesn't share your Faith with the hope that he or she will convert eventually?

To answer these questions—or rather, give you the tools to answer them for yourself—I'll have to share a lot of information, including some hard truths that not every dating book will share. But I think you can handle the truth, even if it's a little hard.

After that, I'll touch on the topic of non-practicing Catholics, as well as the different "tribes" within Catholicism—labels or movements like traditional, charismatic, conservative, liberal, etc.—and whether you should make sure to marry or date someone in the same tribe as yourself. This will be a chapter full of Bible verses and references to the Catechism and Canon Law, but I promise there are some real-life stories and tips in here too!

Some Hard Truths About Catholic Marriage

First, here's a refresher on some of the main facts of Catholic marriage that not everyone in the world agrees with, not even all other Christians. (You'll need to learn all this when you do marriage prep someday, but it's even better to learn it before you're actively planning a wedding, right?)

Lifelong, no divorce

Marriage lasts until death. This means there's no such thing as divorce in God's eyes. To be clear, that doesn't mean that divorce is not allowed. It means there simply *is no such thing*, really—no one can dissolve a valid, consummated (that is, sexual intercourse has occurred), sacramental marriage, not even the Pope himself. "What therefore God has joined together, let not man put asunder," says Jesus in Matthew 19:6. In the same passage, Jesus explains that divorce was allowed by Moses under the old Jewish law because of "hardness of heart," but that "from the beginning it was not so" (Matthew 19:8), meaning that God created us for lifelong marriage. The *Catechism of the Catholic Church* calls divorce a "plague on society" because it damages the image of Christ and the Church that marriage is meant to be. (Jesus doesn't leave us for *any* reason, no matter how badly we have sinned against him!) It also harms the deserted spouse and often traumatizes the children (CCC 2384-2385).

The Catholic Church recognizes that people have a right to separate from (that is, stop living and sleeping with) a spouse for a grave reason (e.g., abuse or adultery. See Code of Canon Law, 1151-1155). But, even then, repentance, forgiveness, and reunion is the ideal. A civil divorce in these cases is tolerated if it is the only way to arrange finances or child custody (see CCC 2383). But a civil divorce doesn't do anything to the sacramental bond of marriage. The two people cannot remarry while the other spouse is still alive because they are still married to each other. In sum, you can separate from a spouse who is harming you or your children, but you cannot end a marriage.

Please know that if you come from a divorced family, or have gone through a divorce yourself, I do not say these things to demonize you or your parents! Life in a fallen world is messy, and lots of people experience divorce as a result of difficult circumstances. I bring it up and phrase it so strongly just to clarify Church teaching so that you can make informed choices moving forward. If you do have wounds from your own or your parents' divorce, a good counselor or a support group can help. And if you are divorced, talk to your priest about the situation, whether there might be grounds for annulment, or how to live faithfully as a married but separated person.

What is an annulment?

An annulment, or declaration of nullity, is a statement by the Catholic Church that what appeared to be a marriage was never a valid marriage at all. That is, at the time the two people got married, something was missing that needed to be there to make the marriage real. There are a number of things that can make an individual or couple incapable of a valid marriage (see Chapter Seven for some examples). In an annulment process, the Church investigates to see whether any of those obstacles were present at the time of the wedding vows. If so, the marriage is declared null and void, and both people are free to marry someone else. If not, the marriage stands, even if both spouses regret it (they vowed, "for better or worse," after all).

Unfortunately, annulments have become so common in these messy times that many people are confused and see an annulment as simply a Catholic divorce. But it's actually very different. A divorce seeks to break a contract that was formed. But Catholic marriage is much more than a contract: it's a sacrament. An annulment says that the sacrament wasn't truly received and the bond of marriage was never formed to begin with.

Unfortunately, even though Jesus states pretty clearly in the Gospels that a true divorce and remarriage is impossible for Christians, most non-Catholic denominations have come to accept civil divorce and remarriage as if divorce really did "put asunder" those whom God has joined. I have known some Protestants who do believe that divorce is evil, or at least that it should not be done lightly, but this belief is not universal among Christians.

Fruitful, open to life

Spouses must be open to the children God sends them. This means no contraception of any kind (whether barrier methods, hormones, or surgeries like tubal ligation or vasectomy). It also means none of what are sometimes called "unnatural sexual acts" in older examinations of conscience: that is, anything that causes male sexual climax outside the union of the spouses' reproductive systems, or anything that causes climax but prevents the man's sperm from going into the woman's reproductive system (see Genesis 38:9).

Contrary to popular belief, this commandment to be "open to life" is not just a bunch of arbitrary rules the Church makes to control what people do in the privacy of their bedrooms, or to try to force people to have lots of children. Instead, this commandment is essentially an instruction manual, an explanation of how to respect our own bodies and our spouse's body. God created the genitals of men and women to be united with each other, first and foremost, because we are beings that reproduce sexually. If we spawned asexually like microorganisms, sex wouldn't exist. So the only right way to do it is the original way, the way that (if all the conditions are right) *might* end up creating a baby.

I emphasize the word *might* because women are actually only able to conceive just a few days out of each month, and only in the years between menarche and menopause. This is also part of how God designed our bodies. And some people are infertile, but are still able to marry and have intercourse, and that isn't sinful. The Church doesn't teach that every sexual act must be *capable* of conception—only that every sexual act must be the *type* of action that *would* be capable of conception if all the conditions are right.

As a side note, you may have heard of the twofold purpose of sex—that it has a unitive purpose as well as a procreative purpose—which Pope St. John Paul II elaborated on in *Love and Responsibility* and elsewhere. Of course, sex has meaning and benefit for spouses beyond reproduction. But that unitive aspect will be destroyed if it is artificially separated from the procreative. If one or both spouses purposely holds back their fertility, rather than offering a total self-gift, the whole act loses its meaning (see John Paul II's *Letter to Families*, 12).

The Church teaches that spouses may legitimately refrain from sexual intercourse on fertile days for the sake of spacing births "for a just reason," but must make sure they are not "motivated by selfishness" when doing so (CCC 2368 and 2370). There's no exhaustive list of "just reasons": in *Humanae Vitae*, Pope Paul VI simply says that these grave reasons could arise from "physical or psychological conditions of husband or wife, or from external circumstances" (HV 16). There is some prudence and discernment involved in the decision to track fertility symptoms and avoid fertile days for a while, which means that spouses must communicate well and discern this together, considering the good of the whole family and not just their own desires.

Many non-Catholics, including other Christian denominations, see birth control as not only acceptable, but responsible. Phrases like "safe sex" and "protection" are powerful euphemisms. A friend of mine once shared that her Protestant friends all used birth control in their marriages and were shocked that she didn't use "protection." (Her response: "Why would I need to be *protected* from my husband?") There's certainly some truth to the idea that it is not always the right time to have a child, especially if, for example, previous pregnancies have been high-risk or finances are already extremely strained. But the Catholic Church teaches that there's a big difference between doing the thing that causes conception while destroying the potential to conceive, and simply temporarily refraining from doing the thing that causes conception.

There's a lot more that can be (and has been) said about this periodic abstinence, which is often called Natural Family Planning (NFP). But basically, the teaching is that we are allowed to use our God-given reason and free will in coordination with the normal way that God designed the female reproductive system either to achieve or avoid pregnancy, for good reasons. That's different from introducing something else into the mix—like synthetic hormones that turn off the normal cycle of fertility, or a layer of latex, or a surgery that injures part of the reproductive system—so that we can have the pleasure of sex any day of the month without "consequences." The first way is working *with* the way God made us, and the second way is working *against* the way God made us. For centuries, all Christian groups and even civil law agreed that introducing anything unnatural into the marital act was wrong, but unfortunately, many non-Catholic denominations have now accepted at least some methods of contraception.

Sacramental and supernatural

Finally, not all non-Catholic Christians believe that marriage is a *sacrament* instituted by Christ and administered to the spouses by each other. This fundamental, doctrinal difference underlies the other differences. If marriage were just a human institution, humans could change it or dissolve it anytime. But because marriage is a sacrament,

God is in charge of saying what it is and how it works. We just get to choose whether to receive that sacrament—and the instructions that come with it—or not.

Requirements for Marrying a non-Catholic Christian

If you get engaged to a non-Catholic, there are a number of requirements you and your intended spouse will need to meet. Your Catholic parish should inform you of them when you start marriage prep, but it's better to know about these earlier on so you and your potential spouse can consider them before you decide to get married and start planning a wedding. They might make or break your relationship, but, to be honest, they should. These are important things to talk about as you consider marrying someone, to make sure you're on the same page about what your future life together would look like.

First, the Code of Canon Law (basically the book of laws currently in place in the Catholic Church) says that a marriage between a Catholic and a non-Catholic requires permission from the bishop (Canon 1124). Normally, you request this permission through your parish church when you get engaged and start marriage preparation. Despite how intimidating this sounds, permission is usually granted.

Also, you must be married in the Catholic Church. This doesn't simply refer to getting married in a Catholic church building, although that is part of it. It means being married in a Catholic ceremony and fulfilling all the diocesan marriage requirements. Basically, it means getting married with the Catholic Church's approval and blessing, because the Church has a responsibility to make sure you're aware of the realities of marriage (including its permanency and procreative aspect discussed above). If a Catholic gets married outside the Catholic Church (that is, in a non-Catholic ceremony without permission from the bishop, or by going to the courthouse or Justice of the Peace), the marriage is invalid.

Next up, you must promise to do all in your power to bring up your children as Catholics and must make your intended spouse aware of that fact.

If all of this sounds as if you're not exactly being encouraged to marry a non-Catholic . . . that's correct. The Church tolerates and permits marriage to non-Catholics case-by-case, but it is not encouraged, because of the real danger of the Catholic spouse and the children leaving the Faith as a result.

Does this sound harsh or bigoted? If we consider what it really means to be a Catholic, it's not at all. Being Catholic means believing that the teachings of the Catholic Church are true and important for salvation. If you don't believe that Catholicism contains the truth—and more of it than any other religion or denomination—then why be Catholic? Meeting Jesus Christ and following Him changes everything about your life (or should). And meeting the Church He founded in order to carry on His mission also changes everything (or should). The Catholic Church is not unreasonable to have these parameters for receiving the Sacrament of Holy Matrimony and trying to make sure that Catholics stay Catholic and that children are brought up knowing the truth.

The Catholic Church is also not unusual for discouraging marriage to non-Catholics. In fact, other religions are often stricter. The vast majority of Orthodox Jews make sure to marry a fellow Jew, in keeping with God's prohibition on intermarrying with non-Jews in the Old Testament. The Quran mostly prohibits Muslims from marrying non-Muslims. The fact that the Catholic Church allows marriage to non-Catholics at all is almost surprising!

Those are the requirements the Church has for marrying a non-Catholic. Now, let's consider some of the possible results of this decision after you're married.

What is Marriage Like with a Non-Catholic?

First, how will marrying a non-Catholic affect your children? A 2015 Pew study found that in families where one parent was Protestant and the other Catholic, the children's religion as adults was "a toss-up," and not just a toss-up between Catholic and Protestant. 38% of these children identified as Protestant as adults, 29% as Catholic,

26% as unaffiliated, and 7% as other religions. In other words, if you marry a non-Catholic, even one who's Christian, your children have about the same chance of staying Catholic into adulthood as they do of practicing *no faith at all.*

On the other hand, 62% of children who were raised in Catholic-only families (where both parents were Catholic or only one parent was present) continue to identify as Catholic. So, if you believe the Catholic Church is the true Church and you want your children to have a strong Catholic faith that they carry into adulthood, marrying a fellow Catholic will definitely give them a better chance.

It's also important to consider the impact of the relationship on your own spiritual life and your happiness in the long term (not just during the honeymoon phase). Once someone asked me (rhetorically), "Do you want to marry someone who doesn't go to confession?" It struck me, and I hope it strikes you, enough to make you consider it honestly.

What would it be like to marry someone who doesn't regularly examine his or her conscience, confess his or her wrongdoings, receive forgiveness from the Lord, and receive the extra grace the Sacrament of Reconciliation provides to help the penitent avoid the same sins in the future? It's so powerful, and such a gift of our Catholic faith that practically no one else has (except maybe the Orthodox). What would it be like to marry someone and then immediately receive Jesus in Holy Communion at your wedding Mass while he or she does not . . . or forgo the Mass because he or she doesn't believe in it? The Eucharist is the greatest gift of all, and it is a gift given not for warm fuzzy feelings, but for salvation (see John 6:53-54). Will you ever be satisfied or feel equally yoked if your spouse doesn't accept these gifts, too?

And there's always, *always* the risk that you will slip out of your own faith and lose these gifts yourself. I have heard of some of the most faithful, on-fire Catholics, even one who did mission work and was devoted to daily Mass, marrying a non-Catholic and relinquishing their Catholic faith as a result. It's hard to live with someone you love and respect day after day and not find your views starting to align over time, or at least allow your own to get a little murky and push them into the background. Canon law actually says that the Catholic party intending to marry a non-Catholic must be "prepared to remove dangers of defecting from the faith" (Canon 1125). It's worth considering honestly whether marrying a non-Catholic would be a "danger of defecting" in itself.

In short, you can marry a non-Catholic validly, and some people have very successful marriages this way. I have at least one friend who is still a devout Catholic as an adult, despite her father not being Catholic, and whose parents seem to have a beautiful, happy relationship. But it's not *encouraged* by the Church, for good reasons, so it's something to consider very, very carefully.

Dating a non-Catholic Christian: Not-So-Hard Truths?

On the surface, it makes no sense to date someone you wouldn't marry. So, if marrying a non-Catholic seems unwise, it seems unwise to date one.

However, as I researched this book, I happened across several examples of couples where one member was not originally Catholic, but genuinely converted over the course of the relationship before marrying. Remember Kayla and Rudy from Chapter Two, and Bernadette and Darren from Chapter Six? Both Kayla and Bernadette have been Catholic all along, while their now-husbands were not Catholic when they started dating. So this can work out, but there are some important features of both of these relationships that are worth noticing.

First, the non-Catholic party was somewhat open to Catholicism from a very early stage of the relationship. Rudy's first message to Kayla asked about her Catholicism. He was somewhat familiar with it and already on a spiritual journey. He discussed doctrinal questions with Kayla as they dated; through these discussions and other factors, he ultimately came around to becoming Catholic.

Darren started coming to Mass with Bernadette's family early in their relationship, during their senior year of high school. He eventually fully converted to Catholicism in college. "He made that decision on his own freshman year, which was awesome," said Bernadette.

"There was never any sort of ultimatum or any pressuring me to become Catholic or anything," said Darren. And this is the second feature of these religiously mixed relationships: the lack of pressure.

"I just said, 'I want you to get close to Jesus and go wherever He leads you,'" said Kayla. "And in my head, I knew that that was the Catholic Church, but I didn't say that out loud." According to Rudy's memory, she had originally told him that she would date a non-Catholic, but would only marry a Catholic . . . but later backed off on this to make sure he wouldn't convert just to be able to marry her. They both knew he had to do it for the sake of truth and for God if he was going to do it at all.

Based on these couples' experiences, it might be fruitful to be open to at least one or two dates with a non-Catholic Christian. But during the course of those dates, don't be shy about your own Catholicism, and try to find out whether the other person is at all interested in Catholicism already.

Here's one of the hard truths I promised at the beginning of this chapter: it's probably not wise to get into a serious dating relationship with someone who isn't open to Catholicism at all. If you do progress into a serious relationship, make it clear to your boyfriend or girlfriend what it would mean to marry you (including the Church requirements listed above), so that he or she can discern whether those requirements are things he or she could meet in good conscience.

One of the most important things to discuss will be the topic of raising your children Catholic. My mom has some wisdom on this. (She and my dad both converted to Catholicism, but my dad was the first to take an interest in it, so my mom had to confront the possibility of being married to someone of another faith.) Here's the way she has always put it to me. Someone who is okay with his or her children being brought up in a different faith must not believe very strongly in his or her own faith, or at least, must not think it's very important. If you really believe that your own Church or denomination has the correct understanding of Christianity, you'd want your children to grow up with the right understanding and the best chance at being saved. But if your spouse believes in his or her denomination just as strongly as you believe in Catholicism, you and your spouse will constantly disagree.

In other words, if you marry and become a parent with someone who isn't Catholic, you have two options: marry someone less devout or less zealous in the search for religious truth, or marry someone who's equally zealous but in a different direction than you are. Rather than wait until marriage or even engagement to figure this out, discuss it around the time you're becoming exclusive. It might be tempting to downplay the differences in your beliefs or the importance of the Church's requirements for marriage, but please don't! You won't do yourself or your potential spouse any favors by papering over these important issues.

Of course, if you decide that you're not going to marry a non-Catholic, you shouldn't progress past the exclusive dating stage and get engaged to someone who isn't already Catholic or in the process of converting. It only makes sense to get engaged to a person you're willing to marry as he or she is now.

Last but not least: pray, pray, pray. Pray for the person you're dating to see and embrace the fullness of Christianity, and for clarity in discerning the next step for yourself. Be aware that, no matter how much you're in love with someone, Jesus loves you more and loved you first, so He needs to come first. If you end up breaking up with someone because the relationship isn't compatible with your faith, Jesus has a greater happiness in mind for you.

Non-Christians and Unbaptized People

So far, I've focused on Catholics marrying non-Catholic Christians, but let's touch on marrying a non-Christian too. Two baptized people, even if they are not both Catholic, can contract a sacramental marriage. A sacrament is something that provides grace, or God's life within us. The grace of the Sacrament of Matrimony makes us capable of fulfilling the lifelong commitment of marriage and having unselfish love (charity, divine love) for a spouse even when natural feelings of love fade. Remember when the Pharisees asked Jesus about divorce in Matthew 19? After Jesus explains that God never intended divorce, the disciples say, "Then it is better not to marry." On a natural level, lifelong love is often difficult, nearly impossible, because of our fallen human nature. But with supernatural grace it is completely possible, and even a joy.

On the other hand, marriage for an unbaptized person (Jewish, Muslim, non-religious, or even someone who identifies as Christian but hasn't been baptized yet) is not a sacrament. This is simply because baptism is the foundational sacrament that causes us to be reborn in Christ and gives us the ability to receive all the other sacraments. In a marriage between a baptized and unbaptized person, the unbaptized person is unable to receive the Sacrament of Matrimony and all the graces that come with it, and most theologians believe that the baptized person also does not receive the sacrament in this case (see the Catholic Encyclopedia article on Disparity of Worship). If you were to marry a non-Christian in a marriage that (probably) isn't sacramental, you could be missing out on a lot of graces that would otherwise help you have a happy, holy marriage.

On a related note, St. Paul says in the letter to the Ephesians that a husband and wife are meant to be an image of Christ and the Church: the wife submitting to her husband as the Church does to Christ, and the husband being willing to die for his wife as Christ did for the Church (Ephesians 5:22-33). This is what a sacramental marriage is, because every baptized Christian has Christ within him or her, and every baptized Christian is connected to Christ's mystical Body, the Church. If either husband or wife is unbaptized, the reality of this mystery is simply not present in the same way.

Plus, there's the simple fact that someone who is not religious at all is unlikely to share your beliefs on sexual morality and even the importance of marriage vs. simply cohabiting. If you date someone who isn't Christian, you'll probably need to have even more conversations even earlier about all this, and you'll have to be very, very firm in your own boundaries and beliefs.

Matchmaker Cristina Pineda recommends not going on more than one date with someone who isn't Christian. It might be okay to go on a date without knowing whether or not someone is Christian, but you can find this out on the first date without getting too personal. Share that you're Catholic and/or simply ask something like, "Are you religious?"

Pineda also told me that if someone is not Christian but interested in Christianity, it's best to introduce him or her to a friend (of his or her own sex) who could provide information about Christianity and be a companion on the journey, but step away from the connection yourself. If you start "evangedating" someone who is so early in the conversion process, you run the risk of putting a lot of pressure on both the relationship and the possibility of conversion.

Non-practicing Catholics

It's very common to meet someone online whose profile says he or she is Catholic, but then to find out on your first date that he or she doesn't go to Mass regularly or seem very knowledgeable about what being Catholic really means. Sadly, this is often a result of poor catechesis and not necessarily the person's own fault.

I recommend treating this situation pretty much like the non-Catholic Christian situation: share how important the faith is to you, stick to your own boundaries on moral matters, and take it one step at a time. You may want to be open to a few dates to feel out what his or her level of interest in the faith really is. But it's probably not a good idea to get official with someone who isn't interested in learning more, coming back to church, and building a real relationship with the Lord—hopefully, for the sake of truth and the Lord, not just for you. If the Lord uses you to inspire someone to come back, that's a gift, of course. But eventually, each person must make the faith his or her own in order for it to be genuine.

You can both work on your spiritual lives while dating, but ultimately, I don't recommend getting engaged unless you have reached a similar level of belief and devotion and can both help each other grow. That's what it means to be "equally yoked."

A Special Note for Women: Male Leadership in the Domestic Church

I already mentioned the verse where St. Paul says that wives should be subject to their husbands "as to the Lord." This has been a difficult saying for Catholics for a long time, especially in our post-feminist era.

One of the primary things to remember is that a wife is called to submit to her husband because the husband is called to die (or at least sacrifice himself in other ways) for her. He is an image of Christ, who died for the Church, His Bride. (I don't know about the rest of you ladies, but the idea of my husband being willing to sacrifice his own comfort or even his life for me doesn't feel sexist—it makes me *swoon*.) He is also called to be the head of their family, a protector and provider for his wife and children in the spiritual realm as well as the physical. (I can't go deeper into this big topic here, but Catholic Answers Magazine has some good articles explaining male headship and wifely submission more thoroughly.)

With this in mind, let's consider what it would mean in particular for a woman to choose a non-Catholic or non-Christian husband.

If you're a woman, consider what role you want your husband to play in the religious practice of your household, and what religious influence you want him to have on your children. Will he participate in family prayers every night, and if so, what do those prayers look like if he doesn't share your devotion to Our Lady or use the Catholic version of the Bible? If your children ask him questions about God and religion, how will he answer? Studies vary on whether fathers or mothers have more influence on children's religion in general, but it's pretty consistent that fathers at least have more impact on their sons' religion than mothers do. Regardless, a man will need to be spiritually healthy himself in order to be a spiritual provider for others. So he ideally needs all the sacraments provided by the Church, especially the sacrament that primarily feeds us spiritually: Holy Communion.

Plus, every child's idea of God is somewhat formed by his or her father, because God calls Himself a father. So it's especially important for women to look for men who can be spiritual father-figures to their children—ideally, men who have the indwelling of God in their souls by baptism and the other sacraments.

Dating Among Different Tribes of Catholics

"Trads" (or devotees of the traditional Latin Mass), charismatic Catholics (or those who emphasize the charismatic gifts of the Holy Spirit in life and worship), conservative Catholics, liberal Catholics . . . sadly, we live in a time where there is a lot of division in the Church between people who think the Church should ideally look, act, and worship in different ways. There is often skepticism or antagonism toward people who think differently. This tribalism (or division, or whatever you prefer to call it) can be a huge obstacle to finding a devout Catholic spouse. Many single Catholics are looking for dates not just among fellow Catholics, but among fellow Catholics of their own tribe, which tends to limit the dating pool pretty severely.

First, I want to validate that desire a little bit. It is important for *spouses* (and therefore engaged couples) to agree on what Mass they will attend and anything else that practically affects their lives. For instance, Catholics at different points on the traditional-to-liberal spectrum might have different understandings of when (if ever) it's okay to use fertility awareness methods (Natural Family Planning or NFP) to space or avoid pregnancies, something that would certainly impact married life. It's also probably a good idea to have some shared devotions so that you can pray together more easily (e.g., you both love the Rosary, or you both love praise-and-worship).

However, I believe it's also very important not to refuse to *date* someone just because he or she appears to be in a different Catholic tribe. There are two main reasons for this.

First, the numbers just won't work. All the time, I hear young Catholic men saying there are no good single women at their parish, and young Catholic women saying there are no good single men at their parish. The obvious solution is that the sexes need to be willing to look outside their parishes (or their preferred movements and activities) in order to find each other.

In my experience, partially backed up by a survey conducted by the Priestly Fraternity of St. Peter ("The Latin Mass Among Millennials and Gen Z: A National Study"), there seem to be more single Catholic men than women in the traditional and traditional-leaning camps, which might help explain why the men and women aren't seeing each other at Mass. So be open to meeting people from other parishes, especially at non-Mass events (e.g., a Young Catholic Professionals happy hour, a diocesan event, speed dating, or unofficial gatherings that happen to include Catholics of different stripes).

At one point, I was limiting myself to meeting men primarily in places where I thought "trad" men would be. God has led me to become very devoted to the traditional Latin Mass over the years, and I wanted a husband who would share that desire for tradition, reverence, and rootedness. But I quickly realized I could not cling to that filter when it came to filling the top of my funnel. I couldn't expect to meet only attractive male clones of myself. So I dropped some of the filters and began to "just meet people" and "default to yes" with any Catholics in the area. I realized I had been limiting my options out of fear that I would accidentally marry someone who didn't share or even respect my traditional devotion. But it's pretty hard to marry someone you don't want to marry.

Interestingly, soon after I let go of my filter and started allowing God to send me whomever He pleased, I went on my first date with Enrique. He had tattoos and wore gauges in his ears and didn't strike me as a "trad" at all. But on our first date, I learned that he actually did share an interest in the Latin Mass: he had discovered it a year or two before as he was reverting back to Catholicism and was affected by its beauty.

I still didn't know whether we perfectly agreed on *every* liturgical question, because there are endless variations of opinion even within a single tribe. But the question of whether we agreed on *everything* became less and less important as it became clear that we agreed on the crucial, practical things: all the official teachings of the Church, the majority of our most important opinions, and even our favorite spiritual practices. It also became clear that God was using our relationship for our betterment. We both continue to learn about Church teaching and liturgy and grow in our spiritual life through our relationship. What else matters?

Time after time, I've observed other couples who went through a similar journey, each learning more and adjusting their habits until they aligned. A woman who grew up in the charismatic movement now attends the Byzantine liturgy with her husband. A woman who was raised more traditionally Catholic married a man who came into the Church through the charismatic movement, and now they incorporate various devotions from both movements into their marriage. A man who grew up in the Society of St. Pius X married a woman who attended typical, "normal" parish Masses. They came to a compromise and now attend Latin Masses at a diocesan parish.

That leads me to the second reason that limiting yourself to people who are already in your own tribe is problematic. This attitude leaves no room for growth in piety and knowledge of the faith, in the other person or in yourself. If you start dating someone from a different tribe, you might both learn a lot and end up naturally aligning. Share your own devotions and views as they come up organically, and be willing to learn about the other person's. You might discover something the Church has to offer that you just weren't aware of before and end up falling in love—with another devotion or form of worship within the Catholic umbrella, if not with your date. Or the same thing could happen to your date, if you joyfully share the devotions God has led you into. Or you might—in fact, you should—*both* learn more about the faith, deepen your relationships with God, and discover more of the riches of Catholic worship together.

Everything was newfangled at some point, even the Dominican order. Every new movement that truly comes from the Holy Spirit has some tradition behind it, even speaking in tongues. Just as it's never a waste to get to know another person, it's never dangerous to *learn* about another person's beliefs and devotions. Just look into what sort of Church approval the movement or devotion has before you start participating and you'll be pretty safe.

People change their opinions *all the time*, before and after marriage. You should marry someone you agree with well enough on all important and practical things, so that you won't be in major conflict from the start. That includes all the *official* teachings of the Catholic Church, at a minimum. But more importantly, you should look for someone who has a "growth mindset" when it comes to the Faith and spiritual life.

Look for someone who is absolutely committed to the truth and has convictions, but is humble enough to recognize that he or she doesn't already know the *whole* truth . . . and become that person yourself.

And again: pray, pray, pray. No matter what tribe you fall into, develop an appreciation for the tradition and authority of the Church. Receive the sacraments of Confession and Communion regularly. Read the scriptures and some spiritual classics like St. Francis de Sales' *Introduction to the Devout Life* and St. Therese of Lisieux's *Story of a Soul*. And develop a real, conversational, personal relationship with God, perhaps with the guidance of a good, trained spiritual director if possible. Give God permission to change you for the better wherever you need to be changed and conform you to Himself, rather than focusing too much on finding someone who conforms to *you*.

9

. . . .

When Should We Kiss?

The Chastity Talk I Wish I'd Heard as a Teen

Finally, the long-promised chapter on physical affection and chastity! If you're reading this book you probably know that sex outside of marriage is sinful and are committed to trying to stay chaste. Excellent! But what about physical affection that's less than sex? Yes, ye olde question: how far is too far?

The advice available in Christian and Catholic circles varies widely. On the one hand, there is the very cautious approach. Joshua Harris and others in the "purity culture" of the nineties advocated for saving your first kiss for your wedding day and having little to no physical contact before that. Harris was a Protestant when he wrote on this topic (and later denounced his books on relationships), but Catholic priest Fr. Chad Ripperger (in his talk "Four Stages of Courtship") similarly recommends couples have zero physical affection before engagement, and moderate affection during the engaged stage.

Growing up, I heard several chastity talks, given by devout and beautiful young women who had come of age during the purity culture phenomenon, suggesting that kissing before marriage was at least dangerous, and that choosing to save the kiss (and possibly hand-holding and other gestures too) was the safer and more praiseworthy choice.

But I also heard talks that indicated there was nothing wrong with kissing when dating, as long as it didn't go "too far," whatever that meant. Amongst ourselves, we teenagers guessed at what "too far" might mean. I remember one friend saying, "You can even make out, just as long as you can handle it." I think by "handle it" she meant, "stop yourself there, and avoid fornication." Easy enough, right?

Even the experts sometimes recommend more affection sooner. In his book *Christian Dating in a Godless World*, Fr. Thomas Morrow says he recommends kissing, hugging, and other gestures of affection before engagement. "Affection is an important language of love, one that should be learned well during courtship," says Fr. Morrow. I also interviewed a Catholic psychologist, Dr. Bryan Violette, to ask about chastity and affection. He said of people who want to save their first kiss for marriage, "I would want to look at that. I would want to explore whether or not there's some fear there, and what their level of comfort with physical affection actually is."

"How far is too far?" someone always asked the chastity speaker at every talk I attended growing up. And the most common answer I heard was, "You're asking the wrong question." The speakers would then explain how we should never seek to go as far as possible without crossing the line into mortal sin, but rather, try to live as virtuously as we can. Naturally cautious teenagers like me interpreted that to mean that whoever touched the least before marriage was the most virtuous.

And yet, I couldn't be satisfied with that answer. How could something as beautiful and sweet as a kiss be so . . . dirty? I couldn't imagine waiting until my wedding day to kiss the man I would marry. But was the fact that I found that difficult just a sign of how lustful I was? Everything I heard and read as a teen and young adult seemed vague and unhelpful.

So I figured some things out by trial and error. I've had relationships that included no affection beyond a friendly hug. I've had relationships that included plenty of kissing. By God's grace, I have avoided premarital sex, but I have not been perfectly chaste in every thought, word, and deed either. I've gone too far, in my own way, but I've also come back and become more chaste, because chastity is a habit you can build, not something you lose forever the first time you slip up. And I did finally find some helpful resources to interpret my own experience and guide me to the virtuous mean between the extremes.

So, with God's help, I'm going to try to be more helpful than any other chastity talk you've heard. I'm going to answer how far is too far. But first, I'll have to lay the foundations by presenting what the Church actually does and doesn't teach, how our culture has distorted us in various ways, and what physical touch does in a relationship. Stay with me for a few more pages of Bible verses and Catechism quotes. I think the end of the chapter will be worth it.

What Does the Church Actually Teach (and Not Teach)?

What the Church does teach

Sometimes, in all the different advice we hear about chastity and dating, we lose sight of what the Church *officially* teaches, so let's start there. As you already know, sexual acts between unmarried people—which are called fornication—are wrong. The Catechism says, "Fornication . . . is gravely contrary to the dignity of persons and of human sexuality which is naturally ordered to the good of spouses and the generation and education of children" (CCC 2353). This teaching is based on the Sixth Commandment, "Thou shalt not commit adultery." While adultery properly refers to a married person having relations with someone other than his or her spouse, the Church has always interpreted this (alongside other Bible verses, such as 1 Corinthians 6:18) to mean that God does not approve of any sexual act outside the union of a husband and wife.

Also, God teaches us that lusting after someone in our hearts, whether or not we commit any external action, is equally wrong. In Matthew 5:28, Jesus says, "Whoever looks at a woman lustfully has already committed adultery with her in his heart." This is related to the Ninth Commandment, "Thou shalt not covet thy neighbor's wife." Although these verses seem to be directed toward men who might lust after women, the Church has always understood that women are held to the same standard: no one should lust after anyone else. The Catechism says that lust is the "disordered desire for, or inordinate enjoyment of, sexual pleasure." It continues, "Sexual pleasure is morally disordered when sought for itself, isolated from its procreative and unitive purposes" (CCC 2351).

So, lust is a desire for or enjoyment of sexual pleasure outside the procreative union of marriage. Lust is evil even without any outward actions because, if you purposely indulge a sexual fantasy about someone you aren't married to, the attitude of your will is exactly the same as if you acted out that fantasy. So it harms your relationship with God just as much as if you committed the same sin externally. It also harms your view of the other person: even if he or she never knows about it, you're still treating him or her as an object for your own enjoyment rather than a person to be loved in a committed relationship.

On the flip side, the Catechism says that the virtue of chastity is "the successful integration of sexuality within the person" (CCC 2337).

There are two main ways to sin against chastity: through external actions, like fornication, adultery, viewing pornography, and masturbation, and through internal acts of the will and imagination, like indulging lustful thoughts. It stands to reason that you could also sin by lustfully touching or kissing someone in other ways, which would be a kind of combination of the two: lusting in your heart, which is already a sin, plus some external action that expresses your lust.

St. Thomas Aquinas backs this up in the *Summa Theologica*, saying that kisses, caresses, etc. are not sinful in themselves if they are done without lustful pleasure, but that they can be mortally sinful if they lead someone to consent to lustful pleasure, or are done for the sake of this pleasure (II-II, q. 154, a. 4).

Similarly, Pope Alexander VII once suggested that a kiss done "for the sake of the carnal and sensible delight which arises from the kiss" is a mortal sin, even if "danger of further consent and pollution is excluded" (Heinrich Denzinger, *Sources of Catholic Dogma*, paragraph 1140). The archaic language is difficult, but he seems to be saying, "It's mortally sinful to use someone for pleasure, even if it's just the pleasure of kissing and you don't go all the way to sex." This makes sense if we consider our internal disposition. If we find a stranger to make out with just for the pleasurable feelings we'll receive, even without any intention of going further, we're using someone for pleasure, rather than loving him or her as a complete person.

And in fact, we can behave lustfully toward someone in one moment, even if we have a loving relationship with him or her overall. Even spouses have to practice chastity, in the sense of loving each other selflessly and remaining open to new life, rather than simply using each other for pleasure.

Related to all this, we need to talk about what it means to be in a "near occasion of sin." You may have heard that phrase at the end of your Act of Contrition or elsewhere. A near occasion of sin is a situation where we are likely to be very tempted to sin. We can never completely avoid all temptation and shouldn't try; if we tried, we'd never be able to do anything. But we should be aware of the situations that are likely to tempt us to sin mortally and avoid them if we reasonably can.

How does this relate back to chastity and touch? As part of growing in chastity and dating well, we need to try to avoid near occasions of the sin of lust, both the external sins (like fornication) and the internal sins (lusting after someone in our hearts). Temptations aren't sins in themselves, but if we notice ourselves being tempted to lust we should have the humility to realize that we might not be strong enough to withstand the temptation, and we should usually try to remove ourselves from the situation by stopping in the moment and setting boundaries for the future.

Every virtue has two opposite vices. If chastity is the successful integration of sexuality within the person, those opposite vices would be two different extremes: first, allowing the desire for sexual pleasure to grow out of proportion and take over our entire personality, or second, shoving sexual desire off to one side because we fear it or feel ashamed of it. Both are equally problematic, because neither option is chastity. God made us to desire sexual intimacy in marriage, so the chaste person does exactly that: looks forward to a happy, holy marriage someday and the pleasure included in that, but does not try to go ahead and have a taste of that pleasure before marriage. (For more on lust versus love in marriage and outside of it, see Dr. Edward Sri's book *Men, Women, and the Mystery of Love*, which is an easy-to-read summary of

St. John Paul II's *Love and Responsibility*.)

What the Church does not teach

There's a tendency among some Catholics to look for rules everywhere, or to hear the opinion of an individual priest, scholar, or layperson and assume that it's Church teaching. This can lead to all kinds of difficulties. So let's mention a few things the Church does not teach.

The Church does not have a comprehensive set of rules for what forms of touch or kissing are permitted or prohibited at different stages of a relationship before marriage. There is no official Church teaching on when kissing is acceptable or what kind of kissing is okay. (When I looked for Catholic resources on kissing, I found a blog confidently proclaiming the opinion that a kiss on the neck is only acceptable from a husband or a fiancé if "your wedding is imminent, i.e., within six weeks or less." I wanted to ask which ecumenical council proclaimed that one!)

For some of us, this feels frustrating: we want precise rules so we can make sure we're not sinning. But that's just not how it works. The Church doesn't say, "Here's how many peanut butter sandwiches you may eat in a day." Instead, she says, "Don't be gluttonous; have self-control in your desire for food and remember that its purpose is to nourish the body." We are called to practice self-awareness and discern for ourselves how many peanut butter sandwiches is too many for each of us, and whether our attitude toward peanut butter is appropriate or approaching a disordered obsession. Similarly, the Church just says, "Don't lust after someone; love people as people, not as objects," then leaves it up to us to apply that principle in our specific situation.

Part of why the Church doesn't have a comprehensive set of rules is that different people will be tempted by different things. Particularly when it comes to the internal sins of lust, some people will happen to be tempted to those by one form or amount of touch, others by another. Even the same people will be more or less tempted at different times. This is why the answer to "how far is too far?" is difficult. As frustrating as it may be, the answer is: "It depends." (But I promise I am getting to some practical principles to help you discern how far is too far *for you*, and even some specific boundaries you can choose to adopt, rather than just resorting to trial and error.)

Thirdly, the Church does not teach that sexual attraction, desire, or arousal are bad. In fact, these are quite good, natural things God built into us.

Arousal in particular seems to cause confusion for a lot of Catholics. There's a notion out there that if we feel arousal before marriage, we must have sinned. On the other hand, there's a reaction against that notion that says arousal isn't a sin, so don't worry about getting aroused with your boyfriend or girlfriend—just don't follow through on that arousal by having sex. But arousal *is* the body preparing for sex, so it is an important clue as we hunt for the answer to "how far is too far?" Part of building chastity—successfully integrating sexuality within the person—is learning to see arousal as a good and natural bodily response to stimuli, but one that can present a temptation outside the right context.

Here is a helpful analogy: when a hungry person smells food, he starts salivating and wants to eat it. If he smells a steak on a Friday in Lent, the salivation and desire to eat become a temptation, even though they are good and normal in other contexts. If someone never feels an appetite coming on when he smells delicious food, something is amiss, even if that lack of appetite helps him fast more easily.

Lastly, the Church does not teach that we are more chaste the less we give physical affection. Sometimes, we mistake the hardest choice for the virtuous choice just because it's hard, or the most counter-cultural choice for the virtuous choice just because it's counter-cultural. But Aristotle said that deeply-ingrained virtue is like a "second nature," meaning that the more we have of a particular virtue the easier it is to act virtuously in that area. And swinging to the opposite extreme from our messed-up culture doesn't guarantee virtue either. We need to learn what chastity really is—sexual desire that is rightly ordered and proportioned—and simply work to bring ourselves in line with that.

Rehabilitating Touch in a Lonely, Hypersexualized Culture

There's another angle to the topic of physical affection: touch is not always sexual or even romantic, not by a long shot. We hold and kiss babies, hug our grandmothers, and shake hands when we meet a new colleague, none of which are remotely sexual actions. But too many discussions of touch in dating assume that all touch between a man and a woman is sexual, or at least constantly in danger of becoming sexual. In a 2018 article in *First Things*, Abigail Rine Favale described a purity talk she heard growing up in the Evangelical movement: "I was asked to imagine myself on my wedding day, in a pristine white dress—and then asked to picture a bright red handprint anywhere that a man has touched me." So if a man had ever tapped her shoulder to get her attention or given her a friendly one-armed hug, she was tainted for her future husband?

Our modern culture is obsessed with sex and tries to make sexual pleasure readily available all the time through hookups, porn, etc. Christian (including Catholic) culture sometimes reacts against this obsession with suggestions that are fear-based and treat the body, desires, and emotions as dangerous or even bad. In a way, it seems that purity culture accepted the same premise as the hypersexualized world—everything is about sex!—but instead of encouraging everyone to indulge in more and more sexual pleasure, it tells people to lock down their desires and tiptoe around on eggshells. In reality, the premise "everything is about sex!" is false. Fr. Morrow describes this problem, then says, "There is a great need to rehabilitate affection in our world, to restore it to its proper place, to purify it of its sexual connotations."

For embodied creatures like humans, touch is an important expression of love, one that single young adults are sometimes starved for. We should learn to love others, and learn how to express this love through touch as well as other love languages, as part of putting sexuality in its rightful place within our whole personality and our relationships.

Can There Be Too Little?

Is there such a thing as too little touch or kissing when dating? Why not stay on the safe side? That's how I used to think, but I've changed my thoughts for a few reasons.

One married woman told me, "It's good to remember that your wedding will, with God's grace, be consummated, and you're going to want to be comfortable with the person, physically, before that." Other married friends of mine agree. It's *not* important to "try out" sex with someone before marriage (that's the objectifying, use-and-discard mentality I've already covered). But it is important to feel safe and comfortable being physically close to him or her.

Plus, being able to touch or kiss a little but not too much, or in the right ways and not the wrong ways, actually takes more self-control and virtue than having an all-or-nothing approach. Therefore, you can better learn your significant other's level of self-control (and your own) by incorporating some physical affection into your interactions.

Dr. Cloud shares in *How to Get a Date Worth Keeping* how a woman who never kissed her husband until their wedding day later found that her husband had some deep sex-related issues. She said, "I don't believe in sex before marriage, but I think if I had at least kissed him when we were engaged I would have instantly known he had some problems."

It's worth mentioning that I also heard from a wife who saved her first mouth-to-mouth kiss for marriage, as did her husband. She didn't regret it. But she also said that they expressed affection in other ways like holding hands, playing with each other's hair, and dancing together. The point is not that everyone must *kiss* at a specific time, but rather, that expressions of affection are a way to get to know someone and can spark important discussions. Use your body language as well as your words to get to know someone, to the level that's appropriate for each stage of your relationship.

Practical Principles: How Far is Too Far for You?

We've laid the foundations. Now, finally, we are ready to talk about some more practical details. Keep in mind that any suggested rules or boundaries I give from here on are simply suggestions for how to avoid near occasions of sin and cultivate the virtue of chastity, not official Church teaching. Consider them, pray about them, and adopt whatever is helpful to you.

Principle #1: *Physical affection should* express *an existing relationship, not* create *an emotional attachment.*

According to the National Institute of Health, skin-to-skin contact of any kind—everything from a baby nursing at his mother's breast to sexual intercourse to holding hands for more than a few seconds—has the potential to cause your body to release oxytocin, a bonding hormone. It's a hormone that makes you feel good and happy and emotionally attached to the person you're touching. This is a good thing that helps human beings bond with each other in all types of relationships, including romantic attachment.

But all good things come with a cautionary note. Because of the bond created by touch, it's important not to start off a romantic relationship with a lot of physical affection. Notice that this isn't so much about chastity—holding hands might give you butterflies and warm fuzzies, but it doesn't normally provide the kind of sexual pleasure that can tempt people into lust. This is more about prudence—if you feel bonded to someone through physical touch, it's harder to break up, even if you have a good reason to do so. It affects your judgment about the other person and how the relationship is going. As one friend of mine put it when she had decided not to kiss a guy too early in their relationship, "Those things can make you love-drunk."

This is also about justice. Although I no longer agree with Fr. Ripperger's encouragement to refrain from all physical affection until engagement, I think the reason he gives for his suggestion is a good one to consider. He points out that creating this attachment in another person, when you could still break up with him or her at any time, is unjust because it causes unnecessary pain. We shouldn't (and can't) avoid all pain and all risk of heartbreak when looking for a spouse, but we can make sure that the level of risk aligns with the level of commitment we have. Your physical bond should develop gradually and organically alongside your intellectual, emotional, and spiritual bonds.

I have a personal example that might help to illustrate both the imprudence and the injustice of too much affection too soon. In one of my past relationships, my boyfriend and I had our first kiss around our third or fourth date. We also began holding hands or sitting close together with arms around each other almost constantly. None of what we did would have looked unchaste to most reasonable outside observers. I was thrilled by the feeling of closeness and the rush of happy hormones I got from this physical affection. But two things happened as a result.

First, we somehow never got around to talking about important things that we needed to discuss in order to discern marriage. It was easier just to sit there feeling romantic and kissing a lot.

Second, when we broke up, I experienced what I can only describe as withdrawal. My body felt physical pain, although I couldn't point to exactly where it was. I fell into depression for months and struggled to keep up a good relationship with God. Not all of that was due to the kissing and cuddling, I'm sure—there were plenty of other things I needed to work on, especially my prayer life—but the sense of withdrawal and how much I missed his touch all the time made it clear to me that something had gotten out of order in that relationship. When other relationships ended that had included little to no physical affection, I was still heartbroken and disappointed but not in the same way or to the same degree.

From my experience of the two near-extremes, I can say that there's a balance to be struck. Slow-rolling your physical affection a little will help encourage you to talk about important things and do the real work of discernment, and you will be able to move on a little more easily if your discernment ends in going your separate ways.

If it helps you, you can choose to set up specific boundaries or milestones for yourself and communicate about them with your boyfriend or girlfriend. For instance, you can follow Dr. Kerry Cronin's advice and limit your touch to "A-frame" hugs in the non-exclusive stage. This is the time when you're building a friendship, and your level of physical affection should probably reflect that: a friendship.

In exclusivity, you have plenty of perfectly chaste options for expressing affection as your relationship gains layers: hand-holding, kisses on the cheek or forehead, putting an arm around your girlfriend's shoulders, and coming up behind your boyfriend to surprise him with a hug. These touches are usually not going to cause a near occasion of sin, and are absolutely delightful. Notice how all of these gestures are closer to what very close friends and family might do. You're becoming closer friends, while also considering becoming family.

Personally, with Enrique, I wanted to save mouth-to-mouth kissing for when we were engaged. This was a choice that worked well for me, to avoid a repeat of the scenario I had experienced before. It also felt beautiful and supremely romantic to have our first kiss right after he proposed, to mark the fact that we were in a new stage of our relationship. But again, this is not a Church teaching. It's also not a complete guarantee against temptation. I could (and did) lust after Enrique in my heart at times before we had ever kissed as well as after, and I repented of that lust and renewed my love for him as a whole person both before and after. I share my choice to save kissing for engagement not to say that you should necessarily do the same thing, but to share an example of what it might look like to build intimacy and commitment on other foundations, then express that existing intimacy through appropriate forms of touch.

As a different example, Kimmie and KJ from Chapter Six had their first kiss on their first date. But their first date didn't happen until they had known each other for a while and discussed many substantial topics, and they kissed after exchanging, "I love you's." There was still a real intimacy that was expressed through the kiss, which is the main point. St. John Paul II makes this point in *Love and Responsibility*: touch should be an expression of the tenderness that the people already have for each other.

Principle #2: You can't have perfect rules, but you can have excellent self-awareness.

In his course *Dating Well*, Dr. Mario Sacasa has a great analogy for physical touch and chastity. He uses the example of drinking, which I'll paraphrase and use here. Let's suppose that five beers will get you drunk. (Becoming drunk to the point that your reason is impaired, on purpose, is a mortal sin, similar to conscious acts of lust, so the analogy works well.) If that's the case, he says, you shouldn't set your personal limit to four beers; there's too much risk that you will find it hard to stop there and will end up drinking five anyway. You're playing with fire, and you have the wrong attitude: trying to get as far as possible toward drunkenness without actually being drunk. Instead, you should set your personal limit to perhaps two beers, so there's a buffer zone. If you drink a third once in a while, you'll be well clear of mortal sin.

With physical affection, the "five beers" are the point at which, as Dr. Sacasa puts it, you're so aroused that it's practically impossible that you won't commit some sin, either going through with having sex or stimulating yourself in some other way to get relief. That is most *definitely* too far! A good "two-beer" limit might be limiting yourself to a few brief, simple kisses when saying goodbye. If you occasionally linger in the kissing a little longer and start to sense arousal (getting into the three-beer zone), you still have time to back off and remain in control of yourself, without consenting to lustful pleasure.

Again, this is simply an example of what a good limit might look like, not a rule you must follow. However, I think it's a limit that would work well for a lot of people. One married woman, whom I'll call Danielle, shared with me that she and her husband instituted a "three-kiss rule" before they were married: no more than three consecutive kisses at any one time. For them, it was a helpful boundary to make sure they didn't spiral into a heavy makeout session that would present a temptation.

Some people say you need to get drunk or close to drunk a time or two in order to "know your limits." Is that true, for drinking or for affection? I don't think so. I think you can know your limits in both areas by practicing excellent self-awareness, paying attention to your body and mind. With drinking, you can be aware of your motor skills, the way you're speaking, etc. and notice when you've started to get a bit tipsy. That's probably a good time to pause your drinking and maybe even stop for the night, while you're still thinking clearly and in control of your actions. Again, that might be after one drink or three depending on your BMI. That might be one drink some nights and three on other nights, depending on how hydrated or tired you are. The best approach is simply to sip your drink at a reasonable pace, stay aware of how the alcohol is affecting you, and actually enjoy the beverage and the conversation, rather than chugging three or four beers in an hour in order to get buzzed and then trying to resist a fifth.

Similarly, when you're expressing affection with your boyfriend or girlfriend, you shouldn't head quickly into a passionate makeout session and then try to stop yourself and him or her when you're already highly aroused and tempted to sin, internally or externally. You should simply express affection—whether it's taking his hand, stroking her hair, a gentle kiss, whatever seems natural. Then, if you feel an urge to keep going further, consider whether you're switching from expressing affection for the other person to seeking sexual pleasure for yourself—at least the pleasure of being aroused, even if you have no intention of going any further.

Recently, Enrique and I had a conversation about times we have noticed this shift from giving to taking in ourselves. It's as if a switch flips at a certain point and the moment suddenly becomes more about the pleasurable feelings than about making the other feel loved; and, at the same time, it becomes *much* harder to stop kissing. He described it as "the animal starting to come out." It's clear to both of us that that's where lust begins, or at least the temptation to it.

So if your switch ever flips, you start to get aroused, and your animal instincts start to try to take over, *that's* your limit—that's the three-beer zone. Set your real limit a step before that, when you're still self-controlled and simply expressing love. Once again, arousal itself is not sinful or bad, but when you're not married and cannot legitimately do the thing that arousal is preparing you for, arousal becomes a *temptation* to lustful acts, whether external or internal. Doing something that causes arousal is putting yourself in a near occasion of sin, which is simply unwise. As Danielle put it, "Arousal is for sexual acts and sex is for marriage, and the wait is more than worth it. We are called to flee from sin, not see how close to the cliff we can get without falling off of it."

When you do get close to that cliff, make sure you have a conversation with your significant other about it. There's no need to get racy in your description of what's going on inside you; just say, "I've noticed that when we do X or Y, it tends to be a temptation for me. Can we stop doing that, please?" Or adopt the simple, lighthearted phrases Danielle and her husband used before marriage: "I don't want you to do a sin," and "That might do me a sin." If he or she really loves you and wants what's best for you, he or she will be willing to adapt and make sure you're not placed in a position of unnecessary temptation again.

A side note: what if everything gets me "turned on"?

What if you find that even the most innocent forms of affection, like holding hands or a brief hug, start to get you aroused? What if even *talking* to someone you find attractive starts to "turn you on"? This is more common than you may think. One Reddit user shared that every time he kissed or even held hands with his girlfriend he got aroused, and asked whether he was sinning: "I really wish it didn't happen because it's frustrating, creates tension, and makes me feel totally guilty," he said. Unfortunately, a lot of us are too embarrassed to talk about this (except perhaps in an anonymous internet forum), so we wonder if something is horribly wrong with us. Or maybe the extreme end of the purity culture spectrum was right after all, that we should never even touch our love interest at all until our wedding night.

I think this is related to the need to rehabilitate touch: many of us are starved for physical affection *while simultaneously* connecting all of it too closely to sex. (Christine Emba and others have written on the phenomenon of "touch deprivation" or "skin hunger" and how it can lead people to seek hookups as one of the few socially acceptable ways to be touched by another person.) And I think depriving ourselves of touch even further is *not* the right answer.

I'm going to get very personal and vulnerable for a moment: I experienced this myself. After trying a relationship with practically no affection, plus living alone and single for a few years, plus coming from a family and culture where physical touch wasn't a primary love language, I found that I was hypersensitive to every touch when Enrique and I first began dating. Without me willing it or even taking any real pleasure in it, I often experienced at least a small flicker of arousal when we touched at all, even in the most appropriate ways, like linking arms.

At first, I felt enormous shame and frustration over this. I was torn between two options: speak up to Enrique, share that even a hug or holding hands was a temptation for me, and risk that he—with his warm, naturally affectionate personality and Latino background—wouldn't be able to handle such a touchless relationship, or else continue forward with this as a cross and do my very best not to consent to any lustful thoughts or feelings.

I took it to prayer and luckily, the Lord had a far better third option. He showed me that I was not so much lustful as in need of healing. My brain and body simply needed to readjust. He guided me to the passages in the Gospel where He healed people through touch and had me meditate on them for a few weeks. After that, slowly but surely, He healed me. I found that hand-holding, hugs, kisses on the cheek, and sitting close together side-by-side became safe, sweet moments of affection, and nothing more. This was possible because Enrique was always self-controlled and respectful, and it was clear to me that every gesture of affection he gave me during that time was a gift, not a way of taking from me. By the time our first kiss on the lips came, I was healed, and it could be what I had always wanted a kiss to be: sweet, romantic, intimate, and innocent. And, it happened right in front of a tabernacle: where God in the flesh dwells, because He took on a body so He could touch us.

So, if arousal seems to be cropping up everywhere, you might need the same course of treatment. You may need to practice healthy affection by easing gradually into the little gestures of affection that shouldn't be arousing you—preferably with family and friends and not *just* a romantic interest, to make it even safer and avoid putting too much pressure on any one relationship—and with a lot of prayer in front of the Eucharist. When in doubt, take a deep breath and ask St. Joseph and Mother Mary to guide you and keep you chaste in thought and deed. They won't lead you astray.

Principle #3: Remember that you can redraw the boundaries anytime

For some reason, I used to feel as if once I had kissed someone I had to keep doing it. The idea of telling a boyfriend, "I decided I actually don't want to do that yet, even though I already did," just seemed too awkward or even unreasonable, especially if the thing in question wasn't *definitely* sinful.

This is just plain false. You can always change your mind. You can always ask for a re-negotiation of the boundaries. You can always communicate your needs and desires. In fact, this is one of the most important relationship skills you can possibly build, because it will help you discern well now and it will be an excellent foundation for communicating in a future marriage.

On her podcast *In the Thicket*, my friend Nicole shared that the conversations she had with her now-husband about kissing and such before marriage were an excellent foundation for communicating about sex within marriage. No matter how awkward you think a conversation about physical affection will be, it's worth bringing up. Danielle agreed: "Have the talk. Being open to uncomfortable discussions will do your relationship a lot of good." Kicking the can down the road and allowing yourself to be drawn into temptation and sin, or even into an unhealthy level of discomfort, will only set the precedent for continuing to avoid this type of conversation in the future.

Enrique and I have had several conversations re-drawing physical boundaries in the course of our relationship. Our first boundary conversation was on our fifth date, before we were exclusive: he had only ever asked for a brief hug thus far, but I proactively told him I didn't want to kiss anyone on the lips again until I got engaged. It felt a little scary to present him with such an extreme boundary so soon, but he immediately agreed to respect it and seemed unfazed. This was one early sign that he was a chaste and self-controlled man I could trust and feel safe with. I never regretted setting that boundary because it showed me more of who he was.

Two or three other conversations about physical boundaries happened over the course of our courtship and engagement. No matter how awkward or scary I was afraid the conversations would be, our relationship has always ended up better and stronger for having them. Once, I hesitated to ask him to change how he expressed affection to me. He immediately said, "Woah. Whatever is best for you is what I want." Ladies and gentlemen, that's the very definition of love. And I wouldn't know how well he loves me if I had either set aside my boundaries and allowed lust to sneak in, or fled from physical affection altogether. The difficulty of navigating this touchy subject (pardon the pun) has been an enormous gift for our relationship.

Specific suggested *boundaries*

Finally, I want to share some helpful, specific do's and don'ts that you can use as starting points or guardrails as you practice self-awareness and formulate your boundaries.

Dr. Mario Sacasa offers two bare-minimum boundaries in his course *Dating Well*. First, keep all your clothes on. Second, don't touch the "erotic zones" of the body. (If you're in any doubt about what those zones include, consider it as the areas that must be covered by a swimsuit.) Whatever other boundaries you adopt, you should certainly have at least these!

Why? Because removing clothing or touching organs of reproduction are actions that are very clearly precursors to sexual intercourse. If you're doing those things with your significant other, there's practically zero chance that you're not consenting to lustful pleasure. In fact, you definitely wouldn't do those things at all unless you had the *intention* of experiencing sexual pleasure or providing it to the other person. So adopting at least these two boundaries is practically necessary to avoid sin.

Next, I want to offer a suggestion for an additional boundary that many people may find helpful. There seems to be a general consensus that "making out," "French kissing," or "passionate kissing"—whatever you want to call it when you are kissing a lot right in a row and getting your tongue involved—is probably not a good idea before marriage. I've heard this from a number of people, including a moral theology professor. Even Fr. Morrow agrees, despite encouraging affection and even "normal" kissing. Danielle shared that "no tongue" was another rule she and her husband had for themselves before marriage.

It's a pretty common boundary among Catholics who seem to have healthy, chaste relationships.

I think my own experience bears this out, too. There's a type of kiss that isn't just an expression of affection anymore; it's a precursor to something else. The switch flips and arousal starts to occur, for most normal, healthy people, about the time that kissing turns into "making out." The urge to continue and escalate the situation gets very strong. You might be tempted to go all the way to fornication. Even if not, you are probably tempted to use the other person for the pleasure inherent in the makeout session or indulge in lustful fantasies later. A simple kiss or two is usually not a temptation for the average, healthy person, which makes sense if we notice how even most married couples kiss as a greeting or just to show affection when they are not preparing for the marital act. (Also, that type of kiss is socially acceptable in public, while couples tend to want some privacy if they're "making out.")

If you haven't already had experiences to teach you that you need different boundaries, adopting these three—clothing stays on, hands stay away from erotic areas, and kisses don't turn into passionate makeout sessions—is probably a good starting point that will prevent unnecessary temptation while still allowing you to express affection in your relationship and even exercise your chastity muscle to make it stronger.

Beyond that, you can develop any further boundaries you need or want by applying the principles from the previous section of the chapter. Use touch to express an existing relationship, not create an emotional bond. Have excellent self-awareness so you can know as soon as something is becoming too much for you. And remember that boundaries can always be redrawn. If you give your first kiss away, or even your first dozen, and then decide you want to save future kisses for later, that's okay. ("Losing" your first kiss is not like losing your virginity, because a kiss and the marital act are just not the same. And even if you *have* lost your virginity, you can ask to redraw the boundaries and recommit to chastity. God is infinitely merciful.)

Most of all, as with everything in this book: pray, pray, pray! Stay close to the sacraments. Go to confession often, honestly examining your conscience and doing your best to avoid both laxity and scrupulosity when you examine it for sins against chastity. Remember that every sin is forgivable; there's no need to be extra ashamed over sins of lust, any more than sins of gluttony, anger, or anything else. Receive Jesus in Holy Communion as often as you can. Allow Him to provide the affection you need, and ask Him to show you how to love your boyfriend or girlfriend well. Then, communicate clearly and courageously with your boyfriend and girlfriend about what your boundaries are and what might need to change along the way. Whether or not this is "the one," this relationship is an opportunity to grow in the virtues of chastity, honesty, courage, and love of the Lord.

10

. . . .

Wait, What if *I'm* Not the One?

Sudden Vocational Discernment Syndrome and Other Difficulties

When you're dating someone seriously, you usually ask yourself, "Is he or she the one for me?" But as a Catholic who's trying to do God's will, you might also find yourself asking whether you are the one for your significant other . . . or for anyone. In other words, sometime before or during your dating journey, you may question whether you are ready to date or get married, or whether you are called to marriage at all. What if God is calling you to serve Him by staying single?

In Catholic terms, the sense of being called to a particular state in life—priesthood, religious life, or marriage—is usually called a vocation, which comes from a Latin word literally meaning "calling." And the process of figuring out your vocation is often called discernment.

Ideally, the question of whether you are called to marriage at all should be answered before you dive into dating. But life is messier than ideals, and many single Catholics have found themselves halfway to the altar before sensing a call to . . . well, the other altar. And many have been on the receiving end of a uniquely Catholic breakup: "You're great; I just need to discern religious life."

I (half jokingly) call these about-faces Sudden Vocational Discernment Syndrome. Does a case of SVDS mean you really are called to the celibate life or could it just be cold feet? I'll share some tips and resources that can help you answer that question, or even discern better now while you're single so that SVDS won't crop up later when you're in a relationship.

Even worse, many dating people, Catholic or not, get into relationships only to discover that there's some habitual sin, addiction, or wound in either themselves or their significant other that causes difficulties in the relationship and might be an obstacle to a holy, happy marriage.

Why does this happen? Why can't everyone just see their own issues and vocational difficulties clearly on their own *before* starting to date? Well, I'm no psychologist, but it just makes sense: if the end goal of a romantic relationship is total self-gift in marriage, which requires self-revelation, eventually, in the process, you'll reveal things to yourself, too. Sometimes, we're so used to our own issues we don't even know they're problematic until a person with different issues runs into them and points them out.

When you realize your soul or brain needs some work, you might need to take a break from dating to do that work. Or staying in your relationship might actually be fine, even beneficial, as you heal and grow. As always, this is a matter of discernment, with no hard-and-fast rules. But here are some pointers. Again, I'm not a psychologist, but I talked to a few psychologists as I prepared to write this book, as well as experts on vocational discernment. And I have personal experience here that I hope will be helpful.

Vocational Discernment: Choosing Your State in Life

What's the problem with Sudden Vocational Discernment Syndrome? And how should we discern our vocations? First, I'll describe the problem a little more fully. Then, I'll share what the Church actually teaches, and doesn't teach, about vocations and discernment. Finally, I'll provide some of the practical tips and resources I've found most helpful in my own discernment journey.

Spoiler alert: you do need to listen to God's call, but you also get a choice—a real, meaningful, free choice. I'm here to share some thoughts that will help you make a wise, practical choice with confidence and joy.

The problem: over-discernment?

Before Enrique, several guys I dated (whether for one date or for months) ended our connections by saying they needed to discern religious life. At one point, I was ranting to my friends and family about it, asking, "What is it about me that makes men run screaming toward a monastery?!"

But I'm not the only one. As I mentioned in the introduction, I know a woman who experienced four breakups from men who decided to consider priesthood—though most of those times, by the same man who just couldn't decide which path to take. Of course, women experience SVDS too. Years ago, I met a guy who asked with frustration, "Why do all the good people want to be religious? If they all do, there are no good people left to marry!"

But I've also met people who ended relationships to consider priesthood or religious life, then ultimately ended up married after all. Lots of devout, well-meaning people switch back and forth between discernment paths, unable to decide what God wants them to do.

There's a danger that Catholics can use "discernment" as an inarguable escape route from a relationship, a way to mask other issues like fear of commitment. If it's God's will that you break up, your ex can't even be angry with you, right? He or she will have to be angry with God instead, but that's not your problem!

I've also encountered men and women who reflect on how long they have been single and wonder if this is a sign from God in itself. "Am I running from my real vocation? Is God calling me to lifelong singlehood?" they ask. This is another form of SVDS. This line of thought often comes with fear, resentment, or sadness. For the person who really desires marriage but struggles to find someone who will marry them, the thought that God might want them to do the very opposite of what they want is a terrible one. "But if it's God's will, I have to do it, right? At least, I have to do it if I want to be a good person and go to heaven!" the thought goes.

The various forms of Sudden Vocational Discernment Syndrome seem to stem from at least two underlying causes: first, overcomplication of the discernment process and, second, a misunderstanding of how God's will and our choices operate together. Everyone's love story or vocation story is different, and life is always a little messy. But there is a simple, clear way to discern, one that gives due respect to God's will being better and wiser than our own but also honors the free will God gave each of us.

Simplification: what the Church does and doesn't teach

What does the Church say about vocations and discernment? In late 2022, I interviewed Dr. Christopher Lane about his book *Callings and Consequences* for Catholic World Report and asked him about this. Lane explained that the Catholic Church has never had one official concept of vocation. That's right: there's no official teaching on how to discern your vocation. There's not even an official teaching that everyone has a vocation pre-planned for them by God that they must discover.

Instead, there's a long history of different saints and scholars describing different concepts of vocation and recommending different ways to discern. According to Lane, a "vocation" originally meant a calling to monastic life or priesthood. The concept of a *vocation* to marriage came later on. People got married as a sort of default vocation, the normal way of life, and celibate consecrated life was an exceptional path. In fact, the Catechism still says, "The vocation to marriage is written in the very nature of man and woman" (CCC 1603).

Then, for many years, people could be placed into a state in life by their parents—think of children being sent to convents or arranged marriages with foreign princes. (Arranged marriages weren't always *forced*, but they weren't exactly totally freely chosen, either.) People could also resist what was chosen for them: at first, St. Augustine fled from the people who clamored for him to be their bishop, though he did end up as a bishop eventually (running from a vocation, literally?). Amazingly, God worked with all of this. No matter how people ended up in their state in life, God was great enough to make them saints if they accepted His grace.

However, the Church has clarified repeatedly for the last few hundred years that people must choose religious vows or marriage vows freely in order for them to be valid. Dr. Lane told me that this is pretty much the only official teaching the Church has on vocation: that any state in life must be freely pursued, not forced by society or parents. But there is no official guidance on how to make such a choice.

Again, saints have offered various methods. St. Ignatius, who famously wrote on the topic of discernment, suggested that a decision could be made in three different ways: sometimes, God gives the grace of complete clarity beyond a doubt; sometimes, He draws the heart more gradually over a period of time; and sometimes, we must use our natural reasoning abilities to make a choice, then offer the choice to God in prayer and see whether He confirms it. (For a helpful guide to Ignatian discernment, see Fr. Timothy Gallagher's book *Discerning the Will of God*.)

The common wisdom today generally falls along the same lines as Ignatius's advice, emphasizing prayer, self-examination, and listening to God. Many priests and religious report one of the first two types of discernment experiences described by Ignatius: hearing or feeling God's call at a definite moment, or sensing a more gradual tug in the direction of a particular vocation. Similarly, some married people say they met and knew immediately that something was special about their spouses, while others were drawn to their spouses more gradually. The experience of discerning a vocation is a little different for everyone, because God speaks to each person in the way he or she will understand.

The best discernment advice emphasizes taking action, as well as listening for a call: go ahead and apply for seminary or ask out that girl, and see what God reveals as a result. St. Ignatius described a peace and joy that may come when a good choice has been made, confirming that you are on the right track.

But what if you never hear a clear call, or never have a perfect peace about anything? Is something wrong with you? Probably not. You might just need to make a choice the third way: using natural reasoning and free will. God is powerful enough to work with whatever you choose in good faith. Dr. Lane finished our interview by summarizing St. Francis de Sales's "gentle" approach to vocational discernment: "Don't break your head over it. Make a choice and stick to it, and it's going to be alright."

Free Will: Choosing *a State in Life*

In other words, when it comes to vocation, we have a choice in the matter. Discernment shouldn't be viewed as discovering some secret in the mind of God that He has inexplicably hidden from you. Instead, discernment is more about making a prudent choice between multiple good options, and sincerely seeking God's guidance on that choice.

One of the best resources I encountered when I was considering religious life was a homily (preserved online in written form) by a Norbertine Canon, Fr. Maximilian, entitled "Choose Your Own Vocation." In it, Fr. Maximilian echoes the Catechism by saying that we all have a call to marriage built into our nature. He also points out that Jesus publicly invites His followers to celibacy: "There are eunuchs who have made themselves eunuchs for the sake of the kingdom of heaven. He who is able to receive this, let him receive it" (Matthew 19:12).

In short, Fr. Maximilian argues that we all have *both* vocations—callings to marriage and to consecrated life—and we get to choose! "Is one better than the other? Sure. And maybe that'll influence your choice," says Fr. Maximilian. "But don't stress over it. In the body, the heart is a nobler organ than the liver, fine, but the body needs both not to die."

He does acknowledge that some people are very specifically called to a vocation, giving the example of St. Joseph being directly encouraged by the angel Gabriel to marry the Blessed Mother. And there are many other examples in Church history of people clearly called by God to follow a certain path. All the same, expecting some sort of supernatural sign—a lightning bolt from God—isn't prudent. As Fr. Maximilian puts it, "Don't plan on it happening to you."

Most vocation directors today don't go quite as far as Fr.

162

Maximilian. Most give more credence to the idea that everyone is called to a particular vocation, and that there are probably real consequences to yourself and the Church if you reject His call. But remember, God knows how to speak to you in a way you will understand, whether it's as obvious as Gabriel's message or not. Trust that He will make His will clear to you as long as you have a relationship with Him. And remember that He doesn't violate your free will. He invites you to a vocation, so that you can freely choose to embrace it.

A simple, practical method

Again, there are many ways people seek God's advice and make a choice. But the way I found most helpful came from Fr. Mike Schmitz's video "4 Helpful Rules for Discernment." In the video, he illustrates the four rules as four doors that you need to go through, in order, when considering a particular option. If the first door is closed to you, you can't go through the second, third, or fourth, so you already know to rule out that option. If the first door is open, but the second is closed, same thing. And so forth. Trying the four doors in order requires a healthy mixture of action, introspection, and prayer.

Here are his four doors, with some of my own commentary and suggestions:

1. **Is this a *good* choice?** For priesthood, religious life, consecrated single life, and marriage, the answer is yes, because these are all options that God has provided for us, as we've already mentioned. By the way, it's very helpful to see good examples of happy, holy marriages and of happy, holy priests, religious, and consecrated single people so that you can really accept the goodness of all states in life, without idealizing them.

2. **Is this a *possible* choice for me?** Sometimes, there's an obstacle in your way. For instance, if a religious order has denied your application, entering is no longer a possible choice for you. If the person you were considering marrying breaks up with you and says it's over, the door of marriage to *that* person is probably closed. This is why discernment requires action, not just prayer and thinking. There's always another person, whether a

potential spouse or a vocation director, involved in your decision as well. The only way to find out if a door is open is to walk up to it and try the handle.

3. **Is this a *wise* or *prudent* choice for me?** This is where more of the prayer and pondering comes in. Here, you do need to consider things like how your aging parents will be cared for if you go to the convent, or whether a monastery is the best place for you if you tend toward scrupulosity, or whether marriage and parenthood are compatible with your health problems. Have a conversation with the Lord every day—about everything in your life, not *just* asking Him, "What's my vocation?" Also, talk to wise and holy people in your life who know you well. I know several people, myself included, who took it as a sign from God when well-meaning people told us, "You should consider being a nun/priest!" but they weren't people who knew us well enough to have a basis for that suggestion. People who know you and God well might actually be helpful guides as you discern, but most importantly, *you* need to know God well so that you distinguish His voice from others'.

4. **Is this a choice I *want* to make?** It comes last because it is least, in a way. If the choice is not good, or not possible, or not prudent, you shouldn't choose it, no matter how much you want to. But if the choice is good and possible and seems pretty prudent, but you just don't desire to do this thing, maybe you shouldn't. When all the options are morally good, God *invites* us, but doesn't *command*, and certainly doesn't *force*. He gave us free will and desires for a reason and often uses our good desires to nudge us in the best direction. Fr. Timothy Gallagher, echoing Ignatius, speaks of a freedom and energy that comes when you're on the right path. Especially when we feel several conflicting desires, an abiding peace or sense of freedom can help confirm which path aligns with God's desire for us.

Here's a discernment story of my own. When I had been single for a while after a painful breakup in my mid-twenties, a priest casually suggested I consider a particular religious order. I had really always wanted to be married, but occasionally wondered whether I should give the religious life more thought (only to abandon the idea as soon as a guy showed interest in me). I decided I should really, *really* discern this time, and accordingly signed up for a retreat.

I was blown away by my first retreat with the nuns and immediately decided to become an aspirant: someone who is still in the world but aspires to enter the order, or at least, is strongly considering it. I spent nearly a year as an aspirant, turning down a few dates and trying to focus on God's will alone. The superior of the convent told me I didn't need to worry about them not accepting me. It looked like Door One (Is it good?) and Door Two (Is it possible?) were probably wide open. And as I looked at Door Three (Is it prudent?), I couldn't see any reason why not.

But during this year I became miserable. I wasn't myself. I was gradually becoming an anxious, scrupulous mess. And it was really, *really* hard to turn down those dates. In prayer, I begged the Lord to tell me what to do. But most of the time, when I asked Him what I should do, I encountered only what a friend of mine calls "smiling brick-wall Jesus." If you've encountered it, you know what I mean, and if you haven't . . . well, it's hard to explain. I don't see Him with my eyes, but it's clear that He's there, smiling a little Mona Lisa smile, saying nothing.

Finally, both a close friend and a priest I'd been seeing for spiritual direction separately pointed out to me that I didn't *have* to enter the convent. I didn't seem to *want* to be a nun, and if I didn't want to be a nun, I didn't have to. I had forgotten about Door Four, the Door of Desire! (Maybe because I hadn't watched Fr. Schmitz's video yet.) And I had forgotten that God and His Church tell us to choose out of freedom, with love. Jesus does not want me as a reluctant bride.

So, finally, I contacted the vocation directress (who had been taking longer than expected to review my application, perhaps having doubts of her own after all). I told her I didn't think I was called to religious life. She congratulated me on finding out God's will for me, and that was that. And immediately, I was so relieved, so free! I felt like myself again. I experienced the peace, freedom, and energy that I think St. Ignatius and Fr. Gallagher are talking about, which I hadn't experienced at all as I took steps toward entering the order.

I don't share all this to prevent you from considering religious life, not at all! I don't regret having given religious life a chance, largely because that experience has made me very supportive if any of my children were to go that route in the future. I'm also more confident than ever that marriage is a good choice for me. But I regret the way I viewed God and myself during that time, as if God were a faraway judge who was going to be upset or allow my life to be a miserable failure if I made the wrong choice, rather than a safe, loving Father who was saying to me, "I want you to be holy and happy. We can do that a few different ways. What do *you* want?" He gave us free will for a reason. Remember that love, joy, and peace are fruits of the Holy Spirit. Try taking steps toward a state in life, consider the fruits, and make a choice without fear.

Then, as best you can, *try* not to go back and forth on that choice multiple times. It's hard on you, hard on the people you date, and in some sense, hard on the Church because you're not living out any of the much-needed vocations while you're still deciding. Try to be confident in the discernment you already did, trusting that, if you discerned sincerely, God probably guided you to the right choice already. He doesn't change His mind.

It might be helpful to think of each period of time when you're seriously discerning religious life as if it were a dating relationship, in the sense that you may need some time to heal when the "breakup" happens. Stabilize your prayer life and your emotions before diving into discerning marriage with an ordinary human. Recall who you are, what you already know about yourself, and what God wants of you. Avoid the rebound, and the nasty breakup that might come from it, by pausing to reset.

Similarly, when you go through a breakup, try to take some time before thinking, "Maybe I'm called to be a nun/monk/priest after all." Jesus probably doesn't want to be your rebound either. To the best of your ability, start on a new discernment path from a somewhat neutral, content position. There's no specific length of time to wait, in my opinion. Focus instead on the state of your mind and soul, ensuring you've come to rest and are setting off in a new direction intentionally, rather than being a swinging pendulum.

So, does being perpetually single mean I'm called to the consecrated life?

All by itself, almost certainly not, especially not if you really want to be married. If you are frequenting the sacraments, staying free from habitual mortal sin, praying daily, and using your time in good ways, your desires are probably coming from a good place, so there's no need to *assume* that they are at odds with God's will.

During a particularly difficult "season of singleness" in my own life (shortly before I started dating Enrique), I was praying my rosary, and suddenly, Jesus made it clear that He was with me, *in* me, and that He was sad *with* me that I was still single when I didn't want to be single. It was a beautiful and comforting moment. And yet, I was a little angry, too. "If you're so sad," I asked Him, "why don't you do something about it?" He immediately reminded me that, just as I have free will and He doesn't force me to marry someone, everyone else has free will too, and He doesn't force someone to marry me. It takes two free decisions to make a marriage, and He doesn't force either of them.

Too often, we think He's up in His heaven, *making* everything happen, and we forget that He's also dwelling within us, *letting* everything happen but experiencing it with us. That's why He came down to feel thirst and pain and even go through death for us: to reunite us with Him, so that our wills and His don't have to be opposed.

If it makes you feel better, try a come-and-see visit to a religious order or seminary, and see if it confirms your desire for marriage more fully. Or try a speed dating event or something else related to dating that you haven't tried yet. Maybe the person who will freely choose to marry you is just around the corner after all!

....

Why Not Both?

Everything I've said here assumes that priesthood and religious life are incompatible with marriage. If you've been exposed to a broad range of Catholic traditions, you might have heard that some priests are married. This is true. I don't have space here to explain the Eastern Catholic Churches or the Anglican Ordinariate, but basically, within the Catholic Church there are a number of different particular churches (a little bit like provinces or super-dioceses) that have the same core beliefs but different liturgies, laws, and customs. Sometimes, those laws allow an already-married man to be ordained a priest. In addition, in many cases, married men can become permanent deacons. A whole book could probably be written by someone else about life as a married clergyman or the wife of one. All I will say here is that being a married clergyman, or the wife of one, is a special calling, a sort of vocation within a vocation. This should be discerned carefully as a couple.

For women and men, another option to consider is joining the lay order attached to a religious order (e.g., the lay Dominicans or third order Carmelites). These are lay people who are drawn to the particular charism or spirituality of a religious order and have a relationship with the order, but only follow a few of the practices (such as praying parts of the Divine Office each day) and continue living in the world. Again, this is a sort of "vocation within a vocation" that each person may prayerfully consider.

Being Ready to Date

In his online course *Dating Well*, Dr. Mario Sacasa points out that being ready to date is not the same as being ready to get married, but there are still some things to consider before diving into dating.

More often than not, Catholic and Christian influencers, parents, and mentors seem more concerned with holding single people back from dating too soon than showing them how to date properly. A young woman, responding to a survey I took a few years ago, shared, "I was never given any direction by my parents as to how one goes about finding a spouse other than 'you don't date until you're ready to get married,' which really confused me as a child."

Her parents' directions reflect standard advice in the conservative Christian world, famously promoted by Joshua Harris in *I Kissed Dating Goodbye*. This philosophy says that dating is for discerning marriage, and because dating includes a lot of sexual temptation and risk of heartbreak, you shouldn't do it unless you are ready to get married quickly. I've also heard people suggest specific timeframes, for example, "Don't date at all unless you are ready to be married within two years."

There's some wisdom in this idea, of course. No matter how devout you are, the longer you are in love with someone, the harder it is to resist consummating that love. We aren't made for purely intellectual and emotional long-term relationships with the opposite sex; we are made for marriage and procreation. And even if our relationships stay chaste, the emotional wounds that can be incurred from multiple breakups over the years aren't exactly desirable.

But there are some practical difficulties with the rule "no dating until you're ready for marriage (or will be ready in X years)."

First, it's hard to know when you're ready for marriage. Sometimes, I believe, single Catholics set the bar too high for what "ready to marry" looks like. A man in his early twenties once told me that a lot of his peers believe that a woman doesn't want a man unless he is very well set up financially (e.g., owns a house already or makes a six-figure income). This is actually not true of most of the women I know, especially those in their early twenties; they know that bar is too high.

Whether it's due to this kind of misperception, career goals, mental or physical health, or just not feeling ready, some Catholics avoid dating at all until they are a good way into adulthood. Then, it's a bit of a learning curve to start dating, and it can be a long process of trial and error to find the right person. All of this contributes to a later average age of marriage and fewer Catholics in the "dating marketplace."

The reality is, dating and finding a spouse is usually a years-long process, whether you feel ready to get married when you start it or not. Why not be open to starting that lengthy process sooner?

The second practical issue with waiting to date until you're ready for marriage is that you might just meet someone who seems perfect for you, and if you turn down the chance to date him or her now you might regret it later. Love has a way of changing your life. I know people who have decided to change their career goals, college plans, etc. because they found a person who was better for them than their plans. Sometimes, meeting someone wonderful can be so motivating or so healing that you become ready for marriage quicker than you thought possible. God puts someone in front of you, and if marriage to that person is His will, He can help make it happen.

At this point, maybe you're thinking, "This lady is just arguing both sides and not being very helpful." So I'll make it a little more specific. There are some things that really do make you unready to date. There are other things that might make you not quite ready for marriage, but shouldn't be obstacles to dating. There are a lot of things that fall in the "it depends" category. I'll try to share a few specific suggestions.

Things that usually make you unready to date

Still considering religious life or priesthood

The wise vocation directress at the order I considered joining pointed out to me that if you leave a convent—which is a possibility for several years after entering, just as it is with seminary—you're still free to marry. But if you marry (which is usually not a five-to-twelve-year process like priesthood and religious life), you are no longer free to pursue the consecrated life. So it's better to discern consecrated life first, then, if it's not for you, pursue marriage. If a celibate vocation is still on your mind at all, take steps toward it first and do your best to rule it out before dating.

Occasionally, I hear of people who are considering consecrated life and are told they need to try to date first. From what I understand, this might happen if the vocations director believes that you might be pursuing consecrated life out of fear of the opposite sex or that you need to see a little more of what you'd be giving up before making the sacrifice. If you're told to do it by a competent spiritual authority like that, of course, do it.

But it's probably a good idea to casually mention on a first date that you're still exploring the celibate state of life so your date doesn't get the impression that you're going to get serious quickly. I had one date with a guy who had mentioned wanting to be a monk many times, including on the date. We had a good time and ended up as better friends after that evening of one-on-one conversation. But we naturally agreed there was no sense in spending time one-on-one again after that because of what I discussed in Chapter Four: we weren't going to keep walking down the road. No harm was done, and no hard feelings or awkwardness were necessary because he had communicated upfront that religious life was still on the table.

A prior marriage that has not been annulled by the Catholic Church

Even if you're in the annulment process and practically certain that your previous marriage will be declared null, the Church presumes marriages are valid unless they have actually been proven invalid and declared null. So it's highly imprudent, and arguably immoral, to date someone while in a maybe-invalid marriage. If your marriage is declared null, you are then completely free to date again—without giving your dates the stress of wondering when and whether you're actually going to be free to marry. (Some annulment processes take years.)

An addiction or habitual serious sin

You don't need to be perfectly chaste and temperate to start dating. Everyone is tempted to different vices, and pornography use, drug abuse, and drunkenness are very common sins that many people slip into from time to time. But if the sin has turned into an addiction or a constant habit, it may severely harm your relationship.

Dr. Sacasa encourages people who use porn to consider how it's affecting the relationship. While he says he has seen a healthy relationship be a catalyst for breaking free of a pornography habit, he also shares some questions for reflection.

"Do you have a hard time maintaining lines of chastity because of porn? Is porn being used to hide from difficult conversations in the relationship? Are you using it to mask some shame or other difficult emotions? Are you pressing your girlfriend to act in ways that mimic what you see online?" asks Sacasa.

If you answer any of these with "yes," he says, "I'm going to make a strong appeal for you to consider breaking up." If your answer to all the questions is "no," it's still important to be honest with your significant other about your struggle and to get the support or professional help you need to root out the habit.

If you're dating a person who struggles with porn, Sacasa recommends checking in on the habit about once a month, and breaking up if there's no significant improvement after about six months. Meanwhile, consider whether you feel objectified in the relationship or pressured into sexual activity as a result of your boyfriend's or girl-friend's porn usage. "If you don't see that there's been growth, or you don't feel safe in the relationship, break up," he says.

You can take a similar approach to drug abuse or a habit of getting drunk. Many divorces and cases of domestic abuse are related to substance abuse, so it's important to work on these issues now. Again, get help and strive to overcome the habit, and observe honestly whether the relationship is healthy enough to sustain at the same time. If you or your partner's substance use is causing the relationship to be unsafe or volatile, or the addiction isn't improving over time, it is probably better to end the relationship before it turns into a chaotic marriage.

Being in a time of major transition

Dr. Sacasa points out this one in *Dating Well*. It's not a good idea to start dating when you're going through a big adjustment, such as having just converted to Catholicism, just starting or finishing college, or having just ended a relationship or left seminary. As I mentioned earlier in the chapter, I don't think there's a specific length of time to wait after one of these transitions, and Dr. Sacasa doesn't give a set amount of time either. It's up to you to consider whether you're starting from a stable position—hopefully with a stable prayer routine and some sort of community of friends and family around you. Choose your next step from a stable position, not swinging like a pendulum.

Things that shouldn't stop you from dating

Being unready to have children, and fear in general

Of course, when you get married, you promise to be open to the children God may send you, and the primary reason humans marry at all is to have and rear children. But let's be realistic about how close you are to having a baby when you start going on dates—not very close at all!

The thing that causes babies is sexual intercourse. So following the wise commandment against premarital sex is a good way to make absolutely certain you won't have a baby without having a spouse to help take care of the baby.

God, in His wisdom, also made it take nine whole months to

gestate a baby, and designed women's bodies so that we only have the chance of conceiving a baby for a few days out of each month. In addition, times of high stress can reduce fertility even further. So the chances of conceiving a baby instantly on your wedding night are actually pretty low. All this to say, if you're living chastely, you have *at least* nine months to a year after your wedding day before a baby will be born, and even then, it's usually just one baby, not *children*, plural. Now, working backward, you can't possibly get married in most dioceses until at least four to six months after you get engaged, and you have a lot of choice in how long you date someone before getting engaged. And all of this is without factoring in the possibility of using NFP if you have a good reason to avoid pregnancy when you first get married.

I state all these rather obvious facts because some people say "I'm not ready to have kids" in a way that sounds as if they're envisioning several toddlers being dropped off at their apartment tomorrow while everything else in their lives stays exactly the same. It just doesn't work that way! Realistically, if you go on a first date with someone tomorrow, and you date chastely, you won't have a baby until at least a couple of years from now, and in the meantime, you'll be planning and preparing for the possibility of that baby's arrival. You'll have a lot of control over when that baby comes (even without birth control in the usual sense).

Reservations or fears about the responsibilities of parenthood are totally understandable, because parenting well is so important. But fear isn't a good ingredient when making decisions, and scripture tells us that "perfect love casts out all fear" (1 John 4:18). I was born when my parents were young and not really financially stable, and I've always been grateful that they welcomed me (and several siblings) even though they might not have felt completely ready. God always took care of us and made sure we had what we needed, because He's the real Father of every child. My mom once told me, "If we had waited until everything was perfect, we *might* have had John" (my youngest brother). Instead, John got to have four older siblings, and four more people got to *live*.

For a lot of things, God makes us ready right at the time we need to be, not in advance. Don't let fear of having kids a few years in the future keep you from being open to dating now. In fact, don't let fear of marriage keep you from starting to "just meet people" and be open to dating now. Maybe that's exactly what you need in order to start feeling a little more ready.

The "it depends" category

Age

Despite the legal age for marriage in most places being eighteen, or even sixteen with your parents' permission in some places, our culture has gradually come to a consensus that even people in their early to mid twenties might be too young to get married. At the same time, dating as a teenager is pretty normal in secular culture, because dating isn't really seen as a direct path to marriage.

Some Catholic and Christian circles see this secular model—date young, marry later—and encourage the exact reverse. Marrying young (and having many children) is praised and encouraged, at the same time that parents and mentors discourage dating young. I think it's all well-intentioned—the encouragement to marry young is meant to encourage young people to commit to a sanctifying state of life rather than listening to secular siren-songs about finding one's fulfillment in total independence or having fun before "settling down" (as if marriage has to be the end of all fun!). The discouragement of dating young is meant to save teenagers from a lot of heartbreak and temptation at a time when their ability to make good judgements is still developing. So age really is an important factor when considering whether you're ready to date. But a far more important factor is maturity. Just as there's no specific age at which everyone is magically mature enough to get married, there's no specific age at which everyone should start dating.

Yet another factor is whether or not you've ever met someone you can or should date. Dating someone who is equally mature, virtuous, and self-controlled makes it easier to have a mature, virtuous relationship, which might not be possible if all the maturity and self-control is on one side.

Personally, I think if you're over eighteen and none of the "not ready" factors above apply to you, and you meet someone you're interested in, it's probably a good idea to go on a date, even if you don't feel anywhere near old enough to marry. A lot of first dates never become serious relationships anyway, and those that do take some time, especially if you're following the suggestions from earlier in the book regarding the non-exclusive stage and the friendship-relationship continuum. And a lot of serious relationships don't end in marriage. So, even if you start going on dates with anyone you're interested in now, you will probably be a few years older by the time you are faced with the real possibility of marrying someone. If you wait until you're twenty-five to be open to dating at all, you probably won't be married until later than you hoped.

If you're under eighteen, it's a more difficult question. For any teenagers reading this book, the first rule is to talk to your parents, if they haven't already given you rules for dating. For parents who might be reading this and wondering at what age to let their children start dating, I can't offer any of my own experience here. I didn't happen to date as a teenager and am not a parent yet. But a few things are worth considering.

On one hand, the Church doesn't have any teaching against two teenagers eating burgers together in broad daylight or going to an arcade together on a Saturday afternoon. So, in principle, there's nothing wrong with teenagers going on dates. It's up to parents to judge whether their child and the person they are interested in going out with seem mature enough to behave appropriately.

But, on the other hand, the way most teenagers date now isn't just grabbing burgers with Nikki one day and then seeing a movie with Natalie the next weekend. That norm ended in the fifties, unfortunately. Many teenagers who date fall into the "pseudo-married couple" category, which can certainly lead to a lot of temptation and heartbreak. In a world where so much interaction happens online and through phones, even a teenage couple who doesn't see each other in person every day can be inseparable. Is it possible to overcome these issues by coaching a different way for teenagers to date? Maybe, but it's a Herculean task.

Bernadette and Darren from Chapter Six began their relationship in high school, dated for five years while they attended college, and are married now. When I asked them whether they would recommend letting teenagers date, they both said they didn't particularly recommend dating for so long before getting married, but that they wouldn't tell a couple in such a situation to break up, either. "It's hard, but it can work," was their final word.

Maybe a nice middle ground could be to simply have teens join each other's families for dinner or other activities, or to throw events like dances and game nights for groups of Catholic teens, rather than encourage them to go out on dates alone. As the introduction to this book showed, I've encountered many Catholic young adults who are utterly ignorant of dating etiquette or struggle even to converse with the opposite sex because they didn't receive concrete suggestions and safe ways to practice when they were younger. Providing safe arenas in which to learn the ways of male-female interaction seems important. But again, it's up to each set of parents to consider what's best for each child.

Financial situation

I'll keep this one pretty simple. If you are a man, and you can't afford to cover even simple, tasteful dates, you should not be dating right now. For example, if you can barely make rent and get groceries for yourself, let alone get some clothes that don't have holes and stains, or are going deeper into credit card debt every month just to live, you can't afford to date right now. Dates don't need to be expensive to be nice, but you do need to be prepared to spend *some* money. On the other hand, for men and women, if you have some student loans you're still paying down every month, but you're overall doing fine, that's probably not a reason to hold off on dating (because if you do, sadly, it's probably going to delay your marriage for many years).

Women, please don't expect expensive dates or a debt-free man who owns a home from date one, especially if you're in your twenties and can't afford those things yourself! Not all those things are necessary to get married, much less to start dating.

Mental health and psychological wounds

This is a big topic, so I can barely scratch the surface here. (If you want more, I highly recommend, once again, Dr. Henry Cloud's *How to Get a Date Worth Keeping*, and the book Cloud co-authored with Dr. John Townsend, *Boundaries in Dating.)*

The specifics of each person's situation will be different, but the basic principle here is that you shouldn't date right now if your wounds or mental health issues are causing you to choose people to date who are bad for you, or if dating is making you mentally unhealthy.

For instance, Catholic psychologist Dr. Bryan Violette told me, "We either marry our parents, or we make sure not to." This fits with what Dr. Cloud and others point out, too: a woman who suffered violent abuse at the hands of her father growing up might either choose to date men who are similarly violent, because that's what she feels is normal in a man. Or she may choose to date only men who are the polar opposite: too passive and practically incapable of anger or of being the leader in the relationship. That's just one example of many unhealthy relationship dynamics that can occur if we choose dates based on unhealed wounds.

But awareness goes a long way. If you've become aware of your wounds and have a sense of what a healthy relationship actually looks like, you can be aware of whether your judgment is being clouded by the wound or not. Having other people who can advise you lovingly is also helpful to ensure your wounds aren't choosing for you.

Also, if you choose a good person to date, you will be able to continue healing within the relationship, maybe *because* of the relationship. As my counselor friend points out, sometimes the healing relationship is with a therapist, but it could also be a friend or a love interest or anyone at all. Jesus, the Divine Physician, uses all kinds of methods.

Kimmie from Chapter Six told me that, during her relationship with KJ, after moving to California to live closer to him, she discovered that some childhood trauma was cropping up in her and needed to be dealt with. "We were on this positive trajectory, and I had plateaued because of my psychological state," said Kimmie. She began working with a Catholic therapist and saw a huge difference. I asked them whether they ever thought about breaking off or pausing the relationship so she could focus on healing, but KJ said it never really occurred to him that he wouldn't simply support Kimmie through this difficult time. "We're not called to carry our burdens on our own," said KJ.

This is a good example of someone discovering a wound, working on it in a healthy way (including seeing a real therapist, not simply using her boyfriend as one), and being healed with the support of someone who loved her. Wounds don't always mean you're not ready to date.

But sometimes, they do. One of my former boyfriends broke up with me because he needed to heal from past wounds, specifically related to a previous relationship. As hard as it was at the time, I think he was right. I think both his wounds and some factors on my end had caused us to get into a relationship that was too committed too soon and not built on firm foundations. The relationship was struggling at its core, rather than the wound simply being a manageable difficulty in a relationship that was healthy overall.

Everyone will keep discovering flaws and wounds in themselves, even in marriage, which is part of why it's a sanctifying state of life. But the relationship can't be *based* on a flaw or wound; if it is, it won't be strong enough to withstand the other difficulties that come along. Knowing the difference takes a lot of self-knowledge and prayer, but following a lot of the other advice in this book—slow-rolling your commitment level and physical touch and paying attention to the fruits of the relationship—will help.

One of the many things that showed me Enrique would make a good spouse for me was the fact that dating him caused a lot of healing. That meant that dating him prompted me to discover several wounds in myself, including nasty and deep ones . . . but almost as soon as I could see that they were there, they started improving. I had never experienced that in previous relationships, possibly because I tended to be drawn to men who had wounds and flaws similar to mine.

Enrique is a remarkably mentally healthy person, I think, and whatever wounds and issues he does have tend to be different from mine. This means, by simply being himself, he shows me what healthier and holier looks like in particular areas where I struggle (and vice versa: he says I call him higher, too). God has used him more than once to show me areas I've been damaged, and then it's just a matter of asking God to heal that area. Some things are still healing; others have improved practically overnight. Never once did these issues not make our relationship stronger and better, and never once has Enrique been scared off or disgusted by what is revealed in me. Over and over, he has said, "That doesn't scare me," with a little smile, when I hesitatingly reveal something I'm ashamed of in myself. And when he's told me things about himself he fears will be hard for me to forgive, I really don't find them hard to forgive, because God has already forgiven him, and it's so clear he's striving to be holier all the time.

What's the point of all this gushing about my amazing fiancé? Just that, if only perfectly healed and holy people were ready to date and marry, practically no one would ever be ready to date or marry. It's time to let go of some of the perfectionism about yourself, as well as the people you date. Keep in mind that by dating, you and the other person are each looking for someone you can continue growing and healing with for the rest of your life, because that's a lifelong process. It's sanctification. It's the road to heaven.

11

. . . .

The Engagement Stage

Intensive Preparation for Marriage...
Oh, and a Wedding

Is it true that "when you know, you know"? Not for everyone. Personally, I "knew" I wanted to marry at least two men before Enrique, but it seems they didn't "know" the same about me. I have an entirely different level of certainty with Enrique, but I can only see that in hindsight.

On the other hand, some people never feel they really "know," in this sense of a deep, total, inner certainty. I have one friend who never felt she had complete peace about marrying her now-husband, but that was normal for her—she just tends to feel anxious about major decisions. She chose to get married despite having some anxiety, and she's very happy.

So how do you know you've found "the one"? Or rather, how do you decide that you should marry someone and make him or her the one for you?

You can use Fr. Mike Schmitz's four doors of discernment here, too, and remember that they have to go in order: good, possible, wise, and desirable. If you feel madly in love with someone, so that marriage seems desirable, but he or she isn't an objectively good person, you'll be unhappy in the long run. If someone is an objectively good person, but you don't want to marry him or her, you shouldn't force yourself into it. (Being in love is not at all necessary for a valid marriage, but it's a helpful aid to a happy one.)

You'll have to decide with your whole self. You'll need to use objective facts *and* your feelings, God's input and good advice from people who want what's best for you. Here are some specifics about how to do that, and how to navigate the final stage of a relationship before marriage, the engagement stage. Spoiler: planning wedding details is nowhere near the most important part of being engaged.

How Long to Date

How long should you date before getting engaged? Here are some suggestions from experts and "normal people" I consulted for this book:

- Fr. Ripperger says each stage of courtship should last three to six months, and he lists three phases leading up to marriage. So, counting a three-to-six-month non-exclusive stage and then a three-to six-month exclusive stage, that's six months to a year before engagement.

- Matchmakers Cristina Pineda and Alessandra Conti recommend dating for a year before getting engaged.

- Kayla from the chapter on online meeting told me that her mom advised, "If you don't know within a year that you want to marry someone, you don't want to."

- Fr. Thomas Morrow advocates a two-year courtship before getting married, but says that, at a minimum, there should be no talk of engagement for at least nine months.

Notice how there's a pretty wide range here. I know couples who took three or five years to discern before getting engaged. Some of them were in high school or college when they started dating, so school slowed down their relationship. But at least two different couples I know took a few years to get engaged even in their 30s. One woman who dated her now-husband for a few years before getting married told me that a family member told her, "If it's been this long, and you still don't know whether you want to marry him, it means 'no.'" But ultimately, she said yes and is happy with the choice.

Moving quickly in a relationship might be a good sign: you're both serious about marriage and good at discernment, and the relationship is sailing smoothly. Or it might be a bad sign that you're allowing the initial strong attraction to someone to overpower your better judgment, or succumbing to desperation ("I'm running out of time to have children!"). I know of happy, Catholic marriages—like my soon-to-be in-laws'—wherein the couple agreed to marry within a few months of meeting. I have also seen happy Catholic marriages that began only after years of dating.

So I won't recommend a specific timeline. In fact, focusing on a timeline might even distract you from the relationship itself. If you think you shouldn't date for more than a year without getting engaged, you might start to think at the eleven-month mark, "It's about time to get engaged," rather than asking yourselves, "Are we *ready* to get engaged?" Rather than focusing on a timeline, focus on how well you know each other and whether you still need to answer any questions to make your decision.

Getting Engaged: Discernment Over?

Some Catholic influencers (like Cameron Fradd or Jackie and Bobby Angel) say that engagement is still a part of your discernment. On the other hand, Dr. Mario Sacasa says of engagement, "Discernment is over, and preparation has begun." So which is it?

You're not married until you're married

On one hand, engagement has to allow for some possibility of further discernment, because the final decision to marry happens at the altar. Of course, if anything comes up during your engagement that shows you that marrying this person would be unwise, you can and should *discern* breaking it off. Some people discover real problems in their relationships only by being engaged. Whether it's the diocesan marriage prep program asking tough questions, the wedding planning process, or just the reality setting in that you're about to spend the rest of your life with this person, engagement has a way of highlighting important issues. Those issues should not be ignored.

I've met a few people who have broken off engagements for very good reasons, usually because they were not evenly yoked spiritually. At least one experienced severe depression and anxiety during the engagement, which was a warning sign that something deeper wasn't right. If the relationship is healthy, you might still experience some anxiety about making such a big change in your life, but overall, you should be happy and excited to marry this person. So if something serious comes up—such as a moral or doctrinal incompatibility, severe communication difficulties, or a persistent sense of dread that outweighs your joy—you should absolutely re-open the discernment question. Discern whether there's a real problem or just a case of nerves.

In addition, if you or the people around you notice signs of physical or emotional abuse, this should *never* be ignored, and it's never too late to leave an abusive relationship. And other major moral issues, like deception, infidelity, addictions, or criminal activity, shouldn't be ignored either. One woman shared that she discovered her fiancé was addicted to pornography. After encouraging him to go to therapy and work on the issue, she finally broke off the engagement, just a few weeks before the wedding. "The last straw was finding out that he was lying to me," she said.

This is a great example of a good reason to end an engagement: her fiancé hadn't resolved his sexual addiction *and* he had lied. As Dr. Sacasa says in *Dating Well*, "On your wedding day, you are choosing to marry the person as they are on that day." Please, do not marry someone with the hope that their bad behavior will eventually go away!

Besides simply being harmful to you, abuse or deception that's ongoing before the wedding could make a marriage invalid anyway, if it inhibits your free and knowing consent to the marriage. It is *far* better to get out of an engagement than to go through an annulment.

A promise is a promise

On the other hand, I firmly believe that you should not get engaged with the mindset that you're still *actively discerning*. You're promising to marry someone, causing him or her to make wedding plans, spend money, move, and, most importantly, become more emotionally vulnerable to you. It is unjust and uncharitable to propose or accept a proposal if you know that you still have reservations or need more information to make your decision.

Plus, it will be far harder for you to break up with someone if you discover an obstacle after you have started publicly planning a wedding. Use the dealbreakers and red/yellow and green flags from Chapter Seven, plus a healthy level of input from friends and family who know you well and want your happiness, to discern well before popping the question or answering it.

Think about what a man asks when he proposes. He doesn't usually say, "Will you get engaged to me?" He says, "Will you marry me?" So don't discern getting engaged; discern getting married! Engagement should be the stage when you have made up your mind and are actively preparing for marriage, and only re-entering active discernment if something serious comes up.

. . . .

Meeting the Parents

When should you meet your significant other's family? Different people have different opinions on this, and it partly depends on practicalities, as well as your family dynamics. But I personally recommend meeting each other's families around the time you become exclusive. This prevents you from bringing home everybody you are slightly interested in and perhaps intimidating your date by coming across as overly serious. But it also allows you to incorporate your families' opinions into your discernment to a reasonable degree. It's very, very nice to have your parents' enthusiastic support (whether financial or emotional and spiritual) when you choose to marry someone, and they're more likely to support your marriage to a person they also know and like. The Church says that only the couple has the final say in whether or not they marry, but it's still a good idea to be open to your parents' wisdom and greater life experience.

Plus, it's important for you to know whether you want to become part of your boyfriend or girlfriend's family. Why is there a stereotype that people hate their in-laws? Maybe because people choose in-laws they hate! Discern whether you are comfortable spending holidays with your potential in-laws or allowing them to influence your future children. And think carefully about whether you want to marry someone who probably shares a lot of their traits and habits. We all turn into our mothers or fathers over time, at least a little!

....

If you're uncertain whether something serious has come up—whether your anxiety is a warning sign or just normal nerves—there's a chance you're just getting too caught up in your own head. Try writing down, or recounting aloud to a friend, the actual words and deeds of your fiancé(e) and the story of your relationship, and see if that makes things clear, one way or the other. I can't count how many times describing a relationship or situation aloud to someone trustworthy has clarified it for me, and how many times I have been the recipient of a description and been able to help clarify a situation for someone else. A fresh pair of eyes (or ears) is always a good idea.

When Enrique and I first got engaged, I was happy, but I also had some days of being very anxious and questioning my decision. Soon I realized that I only felt that way when I was alone and thinking about "what ifs." What if we ended up finding something important we disagreed on that we never noticed before? What if it turned out he was somehow deceiving me about who he was, and was really a terrible person?

Notice how vague these concerns are! Whenever I returned to reality and pointed to the way Enrique actually treats me and the fruits I had actually seen from the relationship, I knew that my choice to marry him was still a good one. I could continue down the path that choice had set me on, trusting that the God who had guided me this far would continue to help. Friends and family who knew us well all confirmed our decision even further, because our goodness and happiness together was evident to them. That certainty has been confirmed every month of our engagement as I continue to see goodness in him and good fruits in myself. Now, I'm full of joy and excitement to marry this excellent man I love so much! (Oh, and we have discovered things we disagree on, but they're on the level of whether or not to put a flat sheet on our future bed. Not exactly a major point of doctrine.)

Proposal, Acceptance, and "an Understanding": Communicating about Your Discernment

Most couples don't say they're engaged until there's a ring on her finger and he's formally gone down on one knee. But, because rings are expensive and she might want to have a say in what it looks like, and because it's a terrifying thing (I imagine) to kneel down and ask a woman to marry you if you don't know her answer, most couples have conversations essentially agreeing to get engaged before the formal proposal and acceptance.

In fact, Dr. Sacasa says that, if you have discerned well, a man should know the answer to the question long before he asks it. My dad agrees, but puts it this way: "Proposing is like being a lawyer in court: you shouldn't ask questions you don't already know the answer to."

This is all very good and practical. However, I would caution couples to be very clear in these pre-engagement discussions about your commitment level and where you are with your discernment. I have known couples who openly discussed their plans to get engaged at a certain time in the future, but then encountered big questions and difficulties in their relationships that made it clear they hadn't *both* fully made up their minds yet. This caused a lot of pain and a sense of betrayal that might have been reduced if both people had been a little more precise or reserved in their language.

If you're not sure whether you are going to propose to her, make it clear that you're still making up your mind; try not to accidentally promise to marry her. (I met a man who accidentally got engaged by saying something like, "*Would* you marry me?" True story! But the engagement didn't last.) If you're not sure whether you would say yes if he proposed tomorrow, communicate that you're still making up your mind, at least through strong hints; try not to lead him on to propose if your answer is going to be "no" or "not now."

If you have definitely made up your mind, but there's some good reason to delay buying a ring and printing save-the-dates, you can make that clear, too. But I would say that if you have both made up your minds and had an open conversation about it, you essentially *are* engaged and should relate to each other at that level of commitment, even if the ring comes later. My dad suggests the term "an understanding" for this situation, as in, "They are not officially engaged, but they have an understanding." My point here is, make sure you really do *understand* each other! Whatever label you decide to use for your relationship, be clear what you mean by it.

For myself, I had a history of getting emotionally committed to men whom I really believed were on the verge of proposal, but ended up breaking up with me. (I also, admittedly, have some idealistic notions of ladylike reserve that I've picked up from Jane Austen novels.) So, very early in our dating relationship, I made it clear to Enrique that I didn't believe in giving a man an answer to a question he wasn't ready to ask. And I didn't think a man should lead a woman to believe that his mind was made up if he wasn't actually ready to propose. I wanted the proposal and acceptance to be meaningful and definite, a real question being asked and a real answer being given, and no murkiness about whether or not we had made our decision.

Of course, as our relationship continued, we still had to talk about practical things, like how we would do things if we were to marry each other, and even a general timeline to engagement and marriage. So we ended up using the word "hypothetically" as a signal that we were going to talk about those things, but without promising anything prematurely.

For example, at one point I asked something like, "Hypothetically, if we get married, would you want to have a wedding before or after you graduate from nursing school?" In the spring, he even said something like, "Hypothetically, if we got engaged this summer . . ." which signaled to me that he was pretty close to a decision, if not decided already. So I needed to either come to a decision myself or communicate clearly that I needed more time. It's not a system that would work for everyone, but this is one way to keep your commitment level clear.

Some men like for their ladies to choose a ring and know that the proposal is coming, some like to have her share some ideas and let him make the final choice of ring and time, and some like to surprise them completely. I think a man who wants to surprise his lady should at least probe a little to see whether she wants to be surprised, so that the proposal is not an unpleasant bombshell for either of them.

While we're at it: ladies, know your accurate ring size for the ring finger of your left hand, and let a close friend or two know it well in advance, just in case! I learned this the hard way and had to give my friend Margaret my best guess when she probed for a ring size to give Enrique.

Also, I personally don't recommend a public proposal, especially a surprise public proposal. There's a lot of pressure to say yes if other people are watching and listening. Even if you're pretty much completely certain that the answer will be yes anyway, it's probably best to keep that pressure off. The choice that is made most freely is most meaningful.

During the Engagement Stage: Marriage Prep, Big and Small

Congratulations, you're engaged! First things first: contact the parish at which you hope to get married and ask what they require for marriage preparation. Some dioceses require a class, some a retreat, some just a few meetings with your pastor, and some leave it up to the parish to decide or consider what each couple needs. Most require at least six months' notice to get married in the church, some as much as a year. So it's best to find out what the requirements are and get the ball rolling quickly.

Sadly, most diocesan marriage prep programs are minimal and, by necessity, cater to the "lowest common denominator." Because so many Catholics simply don't know their faith well, and/or are marrying non-Catholics, dioceses and parishes have to start at square one and inform engaged couples about the basic doctrines of marriage that I've already discussed in this book. They usually require a Natural Family Planning course, and they might include some discussion on communication skills and handling shared finances, etc., in hopes of preventing difficulties and divorces later. This is all helpful as a starting point and should be taken seriously.

But as you prepare for marriage, you can choose to do a lot more to supplement your official marriage prep. There are retreats you can go on, like Three to Get Married, and books you can read. But in fact, your whole relationship now is marriage prep, because your habits of communication, prayer, and self-sacrifice—or their opposites— will carry over into marriage. So here are some practical tips for preparing for a happy, holy marriage.

Focus on the relationship, not the wedding

My spiritual director has encouraged me not to make everything functional (that is, focusing every conversation on wedding plans and practical questions) during engagement, but to make everything ultimately about the relationship. She tells me, "Be *present* to each other." It's hard at times, because there's so much pressure to get things done, but it's important. After all, why are you planning a wedding, or finding a new home, or doing any of these functional things at all? Because you love a person and want a lifelong marriage, not just a wedding day.

Remember that marriage is an emblem of Christ's love for the Church. Just as time is never wasted when the Church—including each of us, individually—spends time worshiping the Lord, time is not wasted when engaged or married people simply spend quality time together.

Of course, things do still have to get done, but there's a balance to be struck. To help with this, Enrique and I sometimes plan dedicated wedding-planning dates in which we get together, set an agenda of a few things we want to decide on or do by the end, and knock them out. Usually, one or both of us has done preliminary research on our own so that we have a starting point or a few options, and the "meeting" is quick and easy.

For instance, we planned a date once where we were going to decide on a wedding invitation design. I had looked up an affordable company to order from (shoutout to Canva), and we looked at a few designs and picked one, then adjusted the wording together. We had one or two other items on the agenda, and then we planned to go dancing at a certain time that evening. Having the end time made us both more willing to say, "I'm fine with this" and move on, unless we really had a good reason to quibble. Then, we went dancing and didn't talk about wedding plans a single bit. This system has worked well for us and made sure we have the space to have more important marriage-prep conversations—about children, intimacy, family dynamics, etc.—rather than just wedding-prep conversations.

Keep wedding plans simple, or, remember you're a peasant

One thing that helps you stay focused on your marriage rather than your wedding is keeping your wedding plans as simple as possible. This is also a tip from my spiritual director, as well as my parents, and something that has been proven through my experience. My spiritual director says, "Things will complicate themselves. Always ask yourself, 'What's more simple? What's more peaceful?'"

If you've been to a lot of weddings, think about what details of those weddings you remember positively. Unless you're a professional event planner or a particularly detail-oriented person, you probably forget everything, except the general feeling of being happy and having a good time. So, for your own wedding, don't sweat over details that no one will remember. Just make sure you will have a valid sacramental marriage and be well prepared to receive all the graces you can!

I jokingly call this the "remember you're a peasant" principle. If you're reading this book, you're probably not royalty. If you're not royalty, you don't need a royal wedding. You don't need a weeklong bachelorette trip or matching monogrammed robes or a groom's cake or a limousine or a live band. You can choose to have a few of those things if they feel important to you, but you don't *need* them in order to start your happy, holy marriage.

Also, consider what you can afford, whether yourselves or with help from family. My mom gives wise advice: don't ever go into debt for a wedding! That's not a great way to start a marriage, especially if you're going into debt for unnecessary things surrounding the reception. Only the wedding ceremony itself, two witnesses, and the rings are truly required.

Stay chaste and keep it short

The Catechism doesn't really talk about dating or courting couples in any definite way. But as it describes chastity, it specifically calls on engaged couples to live "in continence" (CCC 2350). All the same principles from earlier chapters apply here: sins of lust, whether internal or external, are still sins of lust, even if your wedding day is coming up soon. You can look forward to consummating your marriage and hope to enjoy sexual intimacy on your wedding night, but trying to have a taste of that pleasure now is still disordered.

The line can be hard to draw, especially when it comes to thoughts and words. But I think this is a pretty good rule of thumb: do your best not to *purposely encourage* thoughts that fixate on the pleasure you'll *receive* from your soon-to-be spouse. Instead, prepare yourself to *give* yourself totally to your spouse. If you're pestered by fantasies that tempt you to lust, turn to God and ask Him what He thinks of what's going on in your mind. You can never go wrong by turning it into a conversation with Him. Ask for the grace to love your fiancé(e) unselfishly. You can even ask for the gift of an enjoyable sex life in marriage—not a bad thing at all!—and then surrender the details of what that might look like to Him.

Chastity tends to be harder than ever as you get closer to your wedding day and fall more and more in love. For this reason, Dr. Sacasa encourages couples to keep their engagements short, no more than a year if at all possible. A few of my married friends have shared that they felt their own engagements were difficult to get through even if they were less than a year long. Six to eight months, if your diocese allows for it, is usually enough for a couple that is well-formed, certain about their decision, and focused more on the marriage than the wedding.

Build boundaries

Wedding plans can cause a lot of situations where you'll need to set healthy boundaries. Your aunt Ethel might try to persuade you into wearing her hideous wedding gown because that's what all her nieces dutifully do, or your own parents might get offended that you're getting married in your fiancée's home town. No matter how big or small, you'll need to consider what is valid input from people who love you and want what's best for you, and what is an unreasonable request that you need to politely but firmly decline.

The reason this is so important is less to do with the wedding, and more to do with your relationships with your betrothed, his or her family, and your own. As my spiritual director pointed out to me, today the conflicts are about cake and music, but next year they'll be about how to bring up your children. Ultimately, these minor conflicts are tests of your ability to establish a new family unit as two grown adults. Practice setting good boundaries about small things now so that it will be easier to set them with more important things later.

Of course, this doesn't mean you're cutting off your family entirely! Scripture says that a man is called to leave his father and mother and be joined to his wife (Genesis 2:24), so there's a certain physical and emotional departure from your family of origin. But ideally, your two families are also connected to each other by your marriage, and your future children get to have relationships with their grandparents, aunts, and uncles on both sides.

I'll recommend Cloud and Townsend's book *Boundaries* once again, which shows how you can lovingly set limits when you need to, in a way that will actually make your relationships better (because they're more honest) in the long term. For instance, tell Aunt Ethel that you really appreciate her offer of the dress, but you've chosen something else that's more your style. Tell your parents that you understand how much they would like you to get married at home, but that you and your fiancée have already discussed it and made a decision you're both happy with. It takes a little practice if you're a chronic people-pleaser, but it's very freeing!

If you're not a chronic people-pleaser and your tendency is to be abrasive or dismissive of relatives' opinions, you might need to work on the "politely" part of "politely but firmly." Give others' suggestions due consideration—you might find they actually do have a good idea that you want to adopt!—and then *charitably* express your decision.

Build bridges

If you have married friends, you may have noticed that their social life changed a lot when they got married, and especially when they had children. It can be hard to keep up the same friendships at the same depth with people who are now in a different state of life. You might have found yourself gravitating more toward fellow single people during your single stage. You and your fiancé(e) hopefully know each other's friends by now, but you may not have a unified friend group. As an engaged couple, you should start trying to cultivate friendships with other couples, so you don't lose your Catholic community as you marry and start having babies.

This is just common sense, but there's some Church authority behind it, too. Recent popes have advocated for a "catechumenate for marriage" as the new model of marriage preparation. The basic idea is this: catechumens (people who are preparing to enter the Church and receive Baptism, Confirmation, and first Holy Communion) are usually sponsored by someone who's already Catholic and experienced in the faith, so that they have a companion on the journey, before and after they receive the sacraments. Similarly, the popes say, couples should have a more experienced couple to accompany them on the journey before and after they receive Holy Matrimony.

In response to this call, some dioceses and parishes have official mentorship programs set up for engaged and newly married couples. The organization Witness to Love provides a marriage catechumenate program and asks engaged couples to choose their own sponsor couple so that they already have a relationship with them. Whether or not your parish has such a program, you can choose an informal mentor couple, or several, whose marriages you admire and seek a deeper friendship.

My friends Meghan and David, who have been married nearly six years now, told me they were grateful that they always had a good Catholic community around them, including couples who had been through a variety of experiences. Their community came largely through a lay movement they (and I) are involved in called Communion and Liberation. I'm grateful to be in the same community, as well as other overlapping communities—a Well Read Mom book club, a parish, a diocese—that contain plenty of married people whose examples I can emulate.

Enrique and I have also been blessed by happily married couples who came to us proactively, saying, "We want to spend more time with you. We're excited for your marriage and want to support you in it." That support has begun with having us over for dinner, giving us wedding gifts, and throwing me a bridal shower, but in the future, I hope we will support each other through births, illnesses, educating our children, and all the other highs and lows of life. So we're taking them up on it, gratefully!

You lived your well-rounded life as a single person, partly in order to meet other single people. Now you'll need to live your well-rounded life as a couple, making sure you have a social element to that life and aren't just becoming turned in on yourselves.

With God and Your Gut, Again

With this chapter, I've caught you up to the stage of the journey I am in now. In a few days, I'll send this book to my editor, and in two months, I'll be married. You're almost through this book, and I hope my advice, and that of the experts and couples I'm quoting, has been helpful so far. Only time will tell whether my own marriage turns out as happy and holy as I hope! But I trust that it will. In fact, I trust that it will be even better than I can imagine, because everything God does for us is better than we can imagine.

In case I haven't made it clear before, everything up to this point— just meeting people, just getting to know people, deciding to be exclusive, loving chastely, discernment, and finally, deciding to marry someone—must be done with constant communication with God. He knows you better than you know yourself and knows what will make you happy and holy. He is the only one who knows the future and how you and your prospective spouse will change over the years. We can only make decisions with what we know now, and the knowledge He gives us when we ask. He speaks to each of us in different ways, often with a combination of gut feelings and wise advice from others. And He is eloquent even in silence. If you ask and get no answer, maybe He's saying, "You have a choice. What do *you* want?"

It comes down to this: if you have found someone who is objectively good, whose presence causes you to grow and brings out the better sides of you, and whom you enjoy being with and want to marry—in other words, if you've found a pretty, good Catholic—say a prayer and choose! And trust that God is with you, before and after your choice: "In everything, God works for good with those who love Him" (Romans 8:28).

Conclusion

· · · · · · · · · ·

God Won't Show You Gold and Give You Silver

"For I know the plans I have for you, says the Lord, plans
for welfare and not for evil, to give you a future and a hope."

Jeremiah 29:11

One of my housemates, Bethany, shared this saying with me: "God won't show you gold and give you silver." It sums up perfectly one of the biggest things I've learned on my winding road to marriage, and something I want to impress upon you, too.

I always knew intellectually that if God took something away from me, it was because He intended to give me something better. When my first boyfriend ended our relationship, I felt dejected to be back at square one, single and realizing that my dreams of being married immediately after graduating from college would never come true. When my next boyfriend ended our relationship and I was plunged into depression, I remember telling God bitterly, "I know you have someone better in mind for me. But I can't think of anyone better . . . except You."

Gradually, as I healed from that rift, I began to take that idea more seriously: maybe He was the one for me. I considered religious life, weaving new dreams in place of the old ones I'd had all my life:

exchanging, in my imagination, a bride's veil for the black veil of a nun, and engagement and wedding rings on my left hand for a simple band on my right. But I ultimately found myself more miserable than ever before, and then freer than ever before when I set aside those new dreams and allowed the old ones to come back. At one time, I had prayed that my vocation would be settled by the time I was twenty-five. Right as I turned twenty-five, I was breaking up with the convent and plunging back into dating. Here we go again, I thought. Maybe the third time's the charm.

The next man I dated seemed like everything I'd ever wanted. He checked every box, fulfilled every criterion I'd ever dreamed up. I found more and more things to admire in him: intelligence, athleticism, good taste, a passion for truth and moral rightness, interesting career ambitions, the clear ability to be a good protector and provider. He was the physical "type" I'd always liked. He was not only Catholic, but exactly the right "type" of Catholic. He seemed like my ideal man, and he seemed to have been placed in my life at just the right time. Here he is, I thought, the someone who was better for me! God is faithful!

But he started to pull away. Slowly but surely, I became the pursuer—well, to be frank, I became the one holding up both ends of the relationship. I was exhausted, depressed, and anxious. I tried to figure out any other explanation for these dreadful feelings, but the truth was that something in our relationship just wasn't right. I had hoped at one time for a Christmas proposal, and instead I got a January breakup. (The previous breakup had been in January too. I had started to fear Januarys a little . . . an interesting, inverse foreshadowing, as you will hear later.)

I had heard what he said about himself in the beginning, observed him from the outside, and decided he must be the perfect fit for me. From there on, ending the relationship from *my* side, over something as slippery as my *feelings*, didn't even occur to me. Relationships take work, I thought. There are going to be hard moments, but it's worth it for such a good and talented and good-looking man! But I was living in my head. In reality, in my body, in the day-to-day, I was miserable and couldn't explain why. The hard moments were gradually outnumbering the pleasant ones. And the breakup came as a relief. We had a good conversation about it and got closure. I cried hard for a day, told everyone who knew us it was over, and decided to move on.

"I know you have something better for me," I said to the Lord. And this time, it wasn't so bitter. I was given a grace of complete peace, joy, even an unearthly euphoria for a day or two after the breakup. I knew, knew, *knew* that God the Father was catching me in His arms and formulating grand surprises beyond my wildest dreams. This most recent relationship had been so much better and more mature than the one before, despite the difficulties toward the end. The one before had been better in some ways than the one before that. I knew whoever came next would be even better for me. God was raising my standards, teaching me what I could expect from Him as His daughter and a princess of the kingdom. And He was making me worthier of "better" as He went, slowly but surely.

(Let me pause to make it clear that when I say "better," I don't mean that I'm ranking these men against each other in their objective goodness, only that the relationships I had with them were better or worse, for a whole multitude of reasons on both sides. I was certainly not the best option for them, either. Heaven forbid that they or anyone who knows them reads this book and sees them unjustly treated! I pray they all have the happiness I have now.)

The only problem now was this: I thought I knew what "even better" looked like. In fact, I made a specific list of my requirements. He would be of at least a particular height, would have a career I deemed interesting—would in short have all the same good qualities that the last boyfriend had, plus a few more. God wouldn't show me silver and then give me bronze. He'd give me gold, and gold in my mind looked like silver, but just a little shinier.

Now, how would I meet this golden boy? I plunged myself into the Catholic social scene in my city, which I had neglected for a while in favor of my now-ended long-distance relationship. I started a singles' group for my parish that later grew into a diocese-wide unofficial ministry (which is now known as Nashville Catholic Singles). I met some nice guys, some weird and awkward guys. None seemed like my type. I kept going to events: parish picnics, Young Catholic Professionals talks, parties, daily Mass.

A friend invited me to a birthday party and said to dress in the nicest thing you already have in your closet. One guy at that party talked to me for a few minutes, then asked me how old I was. I was feeling sensitive about my age, because I was nearing twenty-seven, and I was utterly single (I could remember my own mother being twenty-seven, after she'd given birth to four children). I felt worn out and old, and very offended—didn't this disrespectful youth from California, with his earrings and tattoos, know that it's very rude to ask a woman her age? Clearly, he was trying to feel out whether I was too old for him or not, and filter me out, dismiss me! Well, he wasn't my type anyway. I answered, mumbling in embarrassment that I was almost twenty-seven. As I remember it, he didn't talk to me much for the rest of the party. Perhaps because I left the table and joined a different one . . . but still!

I turned twenty-seven. The summer brought new energy and new opportunities to meet people. It also brought my first few dates since the breakup. Those were disappointments for various reasons—again, not because those gentlemen are inherently disappointing, but there were mismatches of goals, personalities, and senses of humor. The guys were great in their way, but they weren't "gold" for *me*. The dates triggered a fresh round of grieving for my last boyfriend and my old hopes of being married very young. It was too late for me to be married young—I was nearing the average age of marriage, an average that has been rising for decades. I realized anew that I had to face the fact that, no matter how much I wanted it, I might never be married at all.

That July, I had moments of the deepest sorrow and depression I have ever experienced. It may sound dramatic when I describe how utterly dejected I was over my singleness, but it is true. Friends, if you grieve deeply over your singleness, and then feel guilty for being so hung up on wanting a boyfriend or girlfriend, yet find that you just can't force yourself to be satisfied without marriage . . . you are not alone. We are made for union with a beloved. We are made for love. It's natural.

But please, don't let this natural grief lead you to do any harm to yourself or your future marriage prospects. I understand that temptation, but it's fool's gold and won't really satisfy. One night in that dark July, I looked in my own heart and felt pain indescribable, and

I finally understood why people take to drinking heavily, or looking at pornography, or going out to a bar to find a stranger to sleep with, or even harm or kill themselves. Anything that would distract from or numb that pain, anything that would make me insensible and able to forget it, could have been a serious temptation had God's grace not been powerfully present.

But by His grace, I didn't really want to do any of those things. I barely knew how, and it seemed like a lot of trouble. I have a deeper compassion now for anyone who seeks release in those ways, but for myself, I went to bed and cried a little more and finally fell asleep.

Why am I sharing all this? Because, one year after that very darkest night in July, I had a fiancé and was in the midst of both planning a wedding and drafting this book. God's gold finally appeared; or rather, I finally had eyes to see it.

That July and the next few months after it wrought a change in my heart. I took off my filters. I decided to default to "yes" if a man asked me out unless I had a specific, good reason to say no. Suddenly, I got more dates than I ever had in my life. Running the singles' ministry, which was growing a lot at that time, certainly helped—everyone in Catholic Nashville knew I was single and had a way to contact me. But I had run the ministry for several months with no dates before the turning point in July. I suspect my attitude shift showed through subtly in the way I talked to men, so they sensed I was giving them the go-ahead. Or perhaps it was all just God, deciding I was ready now because I no longer expected my future husband to be "my ex, but better." I was ready for whatever, whomever, God would put in my path.

I went on dates. There were some awkward dates, but there were a lot of fun ones. For nearly the first time ever, I went on dates with more than one guy at once. I stopped clinging so fiercely to any one, and instead simply saw them as people, who might stay or might go, but were worth getting to know for an hour or two regardless.

Some chose not to keep pursuing me. Sometimes that was very disappointing. Sometimes I chose to decline another date. Usually it was an amicable split. Some of these dates came from attending a speed dating event, while also trying to facilitate it. That was insane, but so much fun, too! Between dates, I prayed and journaled and reflected on whether I should continue with each man or not, but while on dates, I tried to simply focus on the one man in front of me and enjoy it.

One of those men was the guy from the birthday party. He had started showing up to some events and always made a point of sitting by me to chat. I decided after meeting him a second time that he was a nice guy after all, but still not my type. Then, I decided if he chose to pursue me, I'd give him a chance, since I was giving everyone a chance unless I had a good reason not to. But, outwardly, I was a bit stiff around him, not wanting to encourage him too much. Between the times I saw him, I didn't think about him at all. Finally, he came to speed dating, amongst all the others. As my friends and I went through the names everyone had written down, we came to his paper.

"He wrote you down. Did you write him?"

"No . . . but I should have. I was writing everyone unless I had a good reason not to, so I should have written him. I just forgot."

"Just say you wrote him."

"I can't cheat and change my names. No one else gets to cheat like that!"

"Oh, just cheat!"

So, I cheated and pretended I had written him down along with a few others, and we told him (well, I told him, in a formal email just like all the others) that he had me as a match.

We went out. I discovered he loved the Latin Mass, had followed his family to Tennessee to live near them, and had a penchant for going down "Wikipedia rabbit holes," just like me. He asked me out again. I told him I needed time to reflect. (I had a few other dates around the same time, and I had decided to set boundaries and give myself time to reflect on each one). After reflecting, I realized he had some important traits I was looking for, and he had been easy and pleasant to talk to. And he had put thought into planning a date I would like: a casual dinner at a local brewery followed by a trip to a bookstore. I decided to follow the "default to yes" principle and Cristina Pineda's advice to continue until you hit "Sudden Repulsion Syndrome." (I had met her a few months before, heard her talk at one of my singles' events, and started listening to the wealth of advice she shares online. If I could point to anyone besides God who brought about that July-to-September change in my heart, it was Cristina.) So, I texted the guy, and we went out again.

And again . . .

And again . . .

On our third date, I let him surprise me with where we were going. He planned a lovely outing to a historic site and a wine tasting. Tattooed California guy had class! But more importantly, he had faith. As we walked the grounds of President Jackson's former home, he shared how he had discerned against priesthood after considering it, casually mentioning the things God had said to him in the process. His personal, conversational friendship with God was evident. So was his love for the Mass and the sacraments—both personal prayer and public worship are so necessary for a complete relationship with God. At one point, he stopped in the midst of what he was saying, smiled up into the sprinkling rain drops, and laughed a little as he said, "I *love* being Catholic!"

The next morning as I sat at my desk trying to work, I couldn't concentrate. Suddenly, the realization burst upon me. I was thinking and thinking about this man I'd been out with yesterday. Oh shoot, I thought. I really like him. The "oh shoot" was because I was afraid of being disappointed yet again, hurt even worse than before. The same old wound of rejection might be carved even deeper by this next blow. But it was a risk I had to take. Love is worth it.

A few weeks later, we were on our fifth date, seeing a Christmas lights exhibit. I had actually pitched the idea for this one: he had already asked me to go on another date with him, and I had accepted, but we had no set plans. I had been wanting to see the Cheekwood lights, and I decided I would rather go with him than anyone else. So I asked if he'd like to make that our next date, and insisted upon buying the tickets. He accepted, but insisted upon driving and paying for dinner beforehand. It was a fair deal. Over dinner, I gave him a little Christmas gift: a gold chain bracelet to signify his consecration to Jesus through Our Lady, which he had just made on the feast of Our Lady of Guadalupe. Afterward, as we walked through the magical garden of lights, we talked about all kinds of things, spiritual, intellectual, humorous. He asked me what I most looked forward to about being a parent. I reflected and shared a few things that came to mind. "How about you?" I asked.

He paused to laugh upward a little again and said, "I hope I have a daughter, so I can take her on dates. I want to treat her well, and show her how a man should treat her."

I fell in love. It was almost audible, tangible. I can point to the definite moment. I knew I was in good hands with this man. If he looked forward so much to having a daughter so he could treat her so well, surely he would treat his wife well too. And maybe I would be his wife.

Luckily, one by one, I had either eliminated all the other men I was seeing, or else we had mutually parted. This one was the best, for me. He was starting to look like gold. Enrique.

When I had said I needed time to reflect, he had respected it and wasn't too pushy. Yet, he kept pursuing, steadily and clearly. When I told him after that fifth date that I didn't want to kiss anyone again until I was engaged, he accepted it, although physical touch was most definitely his primary love language. He told me he would be honored, someday, to get to hold my hand.

In January, he asked me to be his girlfriend. It was easy to say yes.

In June, he asked me to marry him.

He did it like this. My birthday—twenty-eight!—was coming up in a few days. He had reserved a Sunday, well in advance, to give me an all-day surprise date. He is always so good at planning dates. I was eager to go. He took me to Mass. He made me breakfast tacos. (He says he doesn't like cooking, but he happily does it for me.) He took me hiking to a state park we'd had on our bucket list. He'd packed a little picnic. Everything up to now was normal and calm. We got back in the car. "You're really gonna like this next part," he said.

"Should I try to guess what it is?" I asked. "Okay . . . we're going to that tattoo shop!" I joked, pointing out the window. "No, maybe that liquor store!" I thought a minute. "Oh, are we going to a church to pray?"

"That's it!" He knew I would like that.

We turned up at the only parish in the town near the state park, the town his parents live in. He knew the church well. The afternoon Spanish Mass was just getting out of the main church. I thought we'd just slip in for a few minutes. "Actually, I got the key to the old chapel," said Enrique, pulling it out of his pocket, "so that we can have it to ourselves."

My stomach turned over. Was it . . . was he . . . ? The thought that he was planning a proposal had crossed my mind. He had hinted back in April at a summer proposal. For some reason, I'd thought summer must mean (or perhaps should mean) July or August. Shouldn't we have at least six months of being exclusive? Shouldn't we know each other for a year? (I didn't count the April birthday party.) Shouldn't we follow some kind of a formula or structure to make sure we were doing this right? Maybe I just wasn't ready yet. But whenever I'd considered hinting at my unreadiness, or hinting that he shouldn't propose until July or August, I just couldn't. Sometime in May, God had told me pretty clearly that I needed to stop trying to control the situation and just let go: "Trust me."

Now, we were in the chapel. He suggested some silent prayer and then a rosary. I agreed to it, and spent the entirety of both in a state of absolute mental panic. But all my panic and prayers came back to this: "Lord, if there is any reason why I shouldn't marry him, or why I shouldn't say yes to a proposal today, please show me now." Nothing. "Lord, what should I do?"

He flipped the question back to me: "What do *you* want to do?"

He reminded me that when I'd asked Him whether I should be a nun, He had asked me what I wanted and given me a choice. "*Discernment isn't just looking for the right answer. It's making a good decision, remember?*" But I still struggled. I was afraid to make a decision. Maybe I would just have to ask for more time. If so, I knew with complete certainty that Enrique would respect that. But I'd hate to disappoint him that way, when certainly he'd rather have an answer right away. Then again, maybe it was all in my head. After all, he was *totally* the romantic type who'd ask for the key to the historic chapel just to please me for my birthday.

After the rosary, he said he had a letter to read to me. The letter began, "My Sweet Girl, I love you. . . . You've been blessing this Earth for nearly twenty-eight years . . ." He wrote of how much I had added to his world, how funny I was, my sweetness and "warm receptivity." My heart pounded. Just a sweet birthday note from my totally romantic boyfriend? Or something more?

At last, he came to a line that said, "You know in your bones that to love the Lord would be to marry and start a holy family. And I have no doubt that you will be an amazing wife and mother to your future family." At this point, I think I gasped and could breathe no more. It was coming, it was coming after all! I hardly heard the next few lines, as he worked his way around to, "And Rachel, I would love nothing more than to be a part of that. I want to be in your corner, and I want you in mine. Rachel . . ."

In a moment, he had set the letter aside, dropped to his knee before me as I sat in the front pew, and asked, "Will you marry me?"

Dear reader, the next bit will sound very strange. Or perhaps it won't, because by now you know me pretty well. You know that I need time to reflect on things. Through my tears, I said, "I'm sorry, I just need a minute."

"Take all the time you need," I heard him say, so gently and warmly. I shut my eyes. He was holding my hand in one of his, and I squeezed it and shut my eyes tight and stayed that way for, I think, an entire minute. The minute seemed to last an eternity. I needed to allow the reality of what was happening to sink in. I needed to understand that I was about to make the most important decision of my life, the decision to promise to marry someone. I did not want to disappoint my sweet Enrique by asking for a few more months or even days, but I knew he and I both would rather that than the worse disappointment of a broken promise later.

I breathed in and out. I prayed, hard, to Our Lord, who was right before me in the tabernacle, and to Our Lady. I still received no reason not to marry him. I wondered if my very fear and hesitation was a reason. If I wasn't sure, I shouldn't say yes . . . right? But when will I be sure? I realized at last that I had no intention of saying no. It was a choice between yes today and yes another day. So why not yes today? What, after all, were my reasons for thinking I needed more time: to see any more evidence that he was good in himself, and good for me? I knew that already! Or simply the thought that others might think we were going too fast, or that we were breaking some sort of rule by getting engaged a mere seven months after our first date?

In a final flash, I remembered that Our Lady was afraid when the angel came before her and presented her with her vocation. She had a choice, and she chose yes. Despite her fear, despite having no way to see into the future and know exactly to what she was binding herself, she said yes.

I opened my eyes. "Yes."

He joined me on the seat, and we wept and laughed, leaning our heads together. He gave me tissues and we said sweet things, though I don't remember what. At last he asked, "Do you want your ring?" I had forgotten all about the slightly shiny something I'd seen in his hand just before I closed my eyes. "Yes!" I said eagerly, and he slipped it on my hand. It fit pretty well. "How did you know my size?"

"Margaret," he said simply. Margaret was my friend who had gone to the nail salon with me a few months before and casually brought up the topic of rings, a fact I had never, ever considered again since. I laughed and praised Margaret's heroic discretion; he had asked her for my ring size months ago, and she'd had to keep quiet all that time.

At some point, I asked, "Did you ask my dad?" He said he had. "What did he say?"

"He said yes. He gave me an enthusiastic yes." I had already made my choice, but now I felt even more secure in it. My dad could see that he was good, and that I was happy. Reality was a lot better than the swirling anxieties in my head.

Then, at last, Enrique asked, "Rachel, may I kiss you?" That kiss was soft, sweet, close but pure. Jesus was there in the tabernacle, our chaperone. It was wonderful. And, as I said before, it didn't have to be this way, but I am glad it was our first.

I could go on and on and tell you about the rest of that day: how we sipped wine outdoors (because tattooed California man still had class) and he dipped me off the picnic bench as if we were dancing and kissed me again in the sunlight. How we went out to dinner after, and I was, for probably the first time in over a decade (I'm a bit of a foodie), completely unable to eat; my body simply said, "No," and instead, I just tried to let it sink in that the man across from me was now my fiancé. How he taught me the Spanish word for fiancé, *prometido* (or *prometida*, the female equivalent): "It literally means 'promised.'" How we got to visit both his parents and mine that same night, and how it was the happiest time I'd ever had with my family, who were so very excited and supportive.

I could go on and on and on about how wonderful this man is to me, and how much his presence has caused me to heal and grow. And then I could quote him to show that, by God's miraculous grace, I do the same for him. But it would take several more books, and my publisher has allowed me but one.

Enrique is not perfect. But he's objectively good, and he's perfect for me. Perfect enough to make me grateful that I didn't marry right after college, or by twenty-five, because I wouldn't have married *him*. Once, his mother asked me if I wished I had gotten married younger. I confessed that, back when I was twenty-two, I hoped I would marry much sooner than twenty-eight, but now I was glad things had turned out this way. I turned to Enrique, half-joking, and asked, "That was in 2017. What were you doing in 2017?"

He replied, "It depends on whether we're talking about before August or after August." What was so significant about August? He explained that it was the month he had started to come back to Christianity after years of not practicing any faith. I knew, of course, that he had fallen away for a while into nothing, and then into Protestantism, before coming back to Catholicism about a year before we first met. But I had never known the exact timeline. My heart stopped in its tracks.

In August 2017, I had been praying a novena to Our Lady, Undoer of Knots, one of my favorite Marian devotions. I had several intentions for it, but the main one had been my vocation and future spouse. During the novena, I had met that first after-college boyfriend and assumed he was the answer. But the breakup had come in January, and I had gone through my first real heartbreak. I had moved on over the years and forgotten the novena, or when I thought of it, figured I just hadn't gotten a yes that time.

Now, I can see that I did. My dear Blessed Mother let no prayer go to waste. Across the ocean, on a trip to Europe, Enrique was seeing the beauty of the Church incarnate in the buildings of Rome and asking the Christian friends who had invited him to come on this trip about their belief. She brought him home, and brought him to me. Now, the gold bracelet I gave him shows how bound he is to her and her Son, and very soon, before this book goes to print—in January, of all months—a gold ring will show how he belongs to me.

Incidentally, I began writing this book before we were engaged. I referenced Enrique's proposal letter just now to quote it, and I see that he actually mentions the book in it: "You have a love for the Lord that absolutely inspires me. . . . Your devotion, and simply the life you live are evidence of that. Not to mention the book you and He are writing together!" Writing together . . .

Dear reader, I know that this book may not solve your relationship problems. I won't be like Dr. Cloud and boldly guarantee that, if you follow my advice, you'll be dating someone in sixty days. I won't claim that you'll have a spouse in a year. I won't even claim with certainty that you'll marry anyone, ever. Even if you're doing everything right, even if you're a wonderful person, there's no guarantee. When I interviewed Dr. Violette and asked him what he wanted to say, he emphasized how hard it is to wait and wait and not know why you haven't found the love of your life yet. "Allow yourself to feel the emotions associated with 'not yet,'" he said. "That's good practice for the rest of your life. Because this dynamic (of waiting for something) happens between you and God for the rest of your life." No, I won't promise you anything. It is for God alone to promise.

But I will say confidently that God will not show you gold and give you silver. And I will say that I have prayed hard all along that the right words will end up in this book and help someone, at least one person, to build a happy, holy marriage.

That person is likely to be someone like I was just over a year ago, someone who limits himself or herself with a lot of requirements that all add up to silver, not gold. We cannot imagine how much happiness we are capable of with God's grace, in this life as much as in the next. Go out there, start meeting people every way you can, just get to know people, pray, have good boundaries, discern well, overcome fear, and trust completely in God. Go out there and look for a pretty good Catholic.

++++

Acknowledgements

Thank you, first of all, to Vianney Vocations, and my editor, Sam Alzheimer, for giving me the opportunity to write this book. Sam, your encouragement and enthusiasm from day one is the only reason I conquered impostor syndrome and finished.

Cristina Pineda helped so much with this book that she might as well be a co-author. I'm deeply indebted to her for her wise advice that shaped so much of this book as well as my own dating life. I'm sure I wouldn't be married to my wonderful husband now if it weren't for her.

My husband, Enrique Canto, also deserves co-author credit. When I signed the agreement to write this book, he was just my boyfriend. As I drafted and re-drafted most of the chapters, he was my fiancé, giving me encouragement and constructive criticism, and most importantly, teaching me about love by living it. Now, he's the husband of my dreams. Thank you, amor, for continually reminding me that this book is God's project, and He is always successful. Also, I truly can't imagine what monstrosity of a book I would have written without you.

Thank you to all my interviewees, whether I know their names and faces or heard their (deeply personal and sometimes heartbreaking) stories anonymously through an online message or a survey. I hold your experiences with honor, and I pray for you all. Many of those interviewees came to me through r/CatholicDating; thank you to the moderators for allowing me to post questions and interview requests. May your matchmaking threads continue successful! Similarly, thank you to the hosts of The Crunch for inviting me into their Discord server, where I connected with two interviewees who were very helpful for the chapter on chastity and affection.

Thank you to all the experts I interviewed or who provided me with resources, particularly Dr. Mario Sacasa for giving me access to his course; Dr. Bryan Violette for changing my perspective on a few key points; and Mariette Rintoul, Chuck Gallucci, and Eric Niehaus (of Gather—comegather.app), as well as Kayla, Rudy, Amanda, and Chris, for changing my mind about online dating.

Thank you to Phil Mauro and Young Catholic Professionals for inviting me to their conference, which led to many helpful connections, and to everyone there who was willing to talk with me about dating. Thank you to Chad Etzel, whom I met there and spoke with later, and to two other coaches, Meghan Elfelt and Maria Spears Mumaugh, who confirmed that the issues I was seeing with Catholic dating are pretty universal. Thank you also to the editors at Catholic World Report, Crisis Magazine, and OSV News, for allowing me to write articles on Catholic dating that ultimately led to this book, and allowing me to mine the same interviews and resources for both.

Thank you to my spiritual director, Michéle, for all her wisdom about weddings, which largely shaped the engagement chapter. Thank you also to my parents, siblings, and countless friends—especially Gloria, Anne, Margaret, Nicole, and the Joanies—for sharing their experiences, their feedback on the manuscript, their food and company when the writing got tough, and so much more.

Above all, I thank my Father and Mother in heaven, for opening the doors and making a dream come true. I've wanted to write a book since I was six years old, and now it's real.

Works Cited

Center for Applied Research in the Apostolate (CARA). Research organization providing statistics on vocations, marriages, Mass attendance, and more. cara.georgetown.edu

Young Catholic Professionals. Local chapters and a national conference offer spiritual and professional formation and social opportunities to Catholics in their twenties and thirties. youngcatholicprofessionals.org

Hoover, Rachel. "Dating culture crisis fuels Catholic marriage vocation collapse." March 6, 2023. OSVNews.com

Cristina Conti Pineda, professional matchmaker, dating expert, and co-founder of Matchmakers in the City. www.matchmakercristinaconti.com

Cloud, Henry. *How to Get a Date Worth Keeping.* Zondervan, 2005.

"Taylor Swift & Travis Kelce—dating against your type." *Trending with Timmerie*, Relevant Radio. September 28, 2023. relevantradio.com

Bottaro, Greg. "7 Rules for Successful Online Dating." CatholicPsych Institute on YouTube. August 2, 2018.

Padusniak, Chase. "The Catfishing of the Catholic Community." "Jappers and Janglers" blog on Patheos.com. September 12, 2016.

CatholicMatch: dating website with a mission to help Catholics find spouses for sacramental marriage. www.catholicmatch.com

OkCupid: dating website that uses an algorithm to match people based on things they care about. www.okcupid.com

Hinge: dating app optimized for quality dates and meaningful relationships. hinge.co

Catholic Dating Nightmares. Crowd-sourced collection of experiences in the Catholic dating world. Instagram.com/catholicdatingnightmares

Catholic Chemistry: Catholic dating site and app that aims to provide a modern, user-friendly interface and emphasizes starting conversations. www.catholicchemistry.com

Nashville Catholic Singles: speed dating and other events for single Catholics in the Nashville area. nashvillecatholicsingles.com

Hoover, Rachel. "Can Catholic Speed Dating Ministries Boost Falling Marriage Vocations?" OSVNews.com. April 10, 2023

Hot and Holy: speed dating and other events for single Catholics in Michigan. www.facebook.com/HHCYAGroup

AZ Catholic Speed Dating: speed dating events for single Catholics in the Phoenix area. www.instagram.com/azcatholicspeeddating

Denver Catholic Speed Dating: regular speed dating events in Denver and online, and occasional pop-up events in other cities. www.denvercatholic-speeddate.com

Schuchts, Bob. *Be Healed: A Guide to Encountering the Powerful Love of Jesus in Your Life*. Ave Maria Press, 2014.

Hill, Sarah E. *This Is Your Brain On Birth Control: The Surprising Science of Women, Hormones, and the Law of Unintended Consequences*. Avery, 2019. Note: This book is written from a secular perspective, and the author is ultimately in favor of birth control being available despite its consequences. I do not agree with that, but the research she has done showing how hormonal contraceptives affect women is still enlightening.

NaProTECHNOLOGY: A women's health science that monitors, maintains, and restores reproductive health by cooperating with the natural reproductive system. naprotechnology.com

Fertility Education and Medical Management (FEMM): A women's health and wellness program that educates women on daily hormonal shifts to achieve reproductive health. femmhealth.org

National Conference for Single Catholics (NCSC): annual conference giving single Catholics the opportunity to grow and be encouraged in their faith through talks, prayer, and social opportunities. nationalcatholicsingles.com

Dating in the City: podcast hosted by Matchmakers in the City cofounders Alessandra Conti and Cristina Pineda. Found on major podcast platforms. Note: This podcast caters to both secular and religious audiences and contains brief mentions of immoral behavior that might not be suitable for young or sensitive listeners. However, the hostesses are usually advising against such behavior.

Dating Well: online course by Catholic psychologist Dr. Mario Sacasa. faithandmarriage.thinkific.com/courses/datingwell

Ripperger, Chad. "Four Stages of Courtship." Sensus Fidelium on YouTube, August 5, 2016.

The Heart of Dating: podcast, conference, and other dating tools for Christians (not specifically Catholics), hosted by Kait Warman and JJ Tomlin. www.heartofdating.com

The Dating Project. Pure Flix Entertainment and Paulist Productions, 2017.

Cloud, Henry and John Townsend. *Boundaries: Updated and Expanded*. Zondervan, 2017.

Eberly, Sheryl. *365 Manners Kids Should Know*. Three Rivers Press, 2001.

CatholicPsych Institute: uses faith, reason, and science to offer Integrated Daily Dialogic Mentorship as an alternative to typical psychotherapy. catholicpsych.com

Morrow, T. G. *Christian Dating in a Godless World*. Sophia Institute Press, 2016.

Cloud, Henry and John Townsend. *Boundaries in Dating: How Healthy Choices Grow Healthy Relationships*. Zondervan, 2000.

Institute for Family Studies: research and policy organization dedicated to strengthening family life and promoting children's well-being. ifstudies.org

Criticalscience: blog publishing deep explanations of scientific research on various topics with the goal of remaining politically neutral. criticalscience. medium.com

"Avoiding Impurity." Ascension Presents on YouTube. September 13, 2017.

Letter to Families from Pope John Paul II (*Gratissimam Sane*), 1994. www. vatican.va

Pew Research. "One-in-Five U.S. Adults Were Raised in Interfaith Homes," 2016, and "Most U.S. parents pass along their religion and politics to their children," 2023. pewresearch.org

Catholic Encyclopedia, "Disparity of Worship." www.newadvent.org

Catholic Answers Magazine. "Do Wives Have to Be 'Submissive'?" December 10, 2018. "Wives, Be Subject to Your Husbands," July 1, 2004. catholic.com

"The Latin Mass Among Millennials & Gen Z: A National Study." June 5, 2020. fssp.com

Sri, Edward. *Men, Women, and the Mystery of Love*. Franciscan Media, 2015.

Wojtyla, Karol. *Love and Responsibility*. Ignatius Press, 1981.

Emba, Christine. *Rethinking Sex: A Provocation*. Sentinel, 2022. Note: This book is not written within the framework of Catholic doctrine and uses language and details that are not suitable for young or sensitive readers. For those who can handle it, it is an interesting exploration of the problems with hookup culture, including the fact that some people hook up just because they crave touch.

"Purity Culture," *In the Thicket* podcast, October 23, 2023. www.inthethicketpodcast.com

Hoover, Rachel. "Callings, consequences, and vocational crises." Catholic World Report, February 2, 2023. www.catholicworldreport.com

Lane, Christopher J. *Callings and Consequences: The Making of Catholic Vocational Culture in Early Modern France*. McGill-Queen's University Press, 2021.

Gallagher, Timothy M. *Discerning the Will of God: The Ignatian Guide to Christian Decision-Making*. The Crossroad Publishing Company, 2017.

"Choose Your Own Vocation": transcript of a homily given by a Fr. Maximilian of the Norbertine Canons of St. Michael's Abbey, Orange County, California. Found on their website's "Vocations" page under a tab called "A Helpful Homily," last accessed January 23, 2024. stmichaelsabbey.com/vocations

"4 Helpful Rules for Discernment." Ascension Presents on YouTube, February 7, 2018.

Three to Get Married retreats: retreats for engaged couples that draw from Ven. Fulton Sheen's book of the same name. There is no one official organizer of these retreats; they are put on by various parishes, dioceses, and movements.

Witness to Love: virtues-based catechumenate model of marriage preparation that can be implemented by lay people in parishes. witnesstolove.org

Made in the USA
Coppell, TX
08 April 2024

31048343R00125